# Melt with Me

# Contents

# Choose Your Own Adventure for '80s Kids

You are walking home from school. The year is 1983 and you're nine or eleven or thirteen, some awkward age when even the air hurts your thin skin. Maybe it's the hole in the ozone the news is just now announcing, the one eaten away by the hair spray containing all the fluorocarbons. Maybe it's that this year was, like every year before and after the year of your birth, one of anger, or maybe the atmosphere is only as cold as the global climate, the war everyone warns is coming.

But today is a fine fall day. A faint hint of frost hangs in the air. The leaves are lifting from the trees and rattling along the sidewalk, and you suddenly, in a first flash of adulthood, imagine them as the years of your life. So you stand and watch the leaves scuttle away downwind and feel the cold come on and the darkness begin to set in early, and it is in this moment that a man in a van pulls up beside you.

**Do you:**

> Get in the van despite all the times your parents have warned you about strangers, kidnappings, vans?
> Take the candy apple the man offers you but otherwise ignore him?

1

Flee through the nearest backyard and into the woods
behind your house?

Ask a neighbor to call the police?

Ignore the man in the van and run home to all the quiet
emptiness of your house?

**If you get in the van:**

The stranger is, of course, not a stranger—he tells you he knows
your uncle John.

You mean Uncle Jerry? you say.

Yes, the stranger says, Uncle Jerry.

So you get in the van. It is moments like these that all
choices hinge upon. That make us or break us, a saying your
father is fond of. But the man cannot be a stranger because he
knows Uncle Jerry, logic that seems, at the time, irrefutable, but
which will, as the future unfolds, become increasingly suspect.

The man puts the van in drive, and you slowly pull away
from everything you know. The mailboxes are switching past
as you cruise down the once-safe street, the one your parents
have let you walk by yourself since you were six. It will never
be safe after this, but you don't know that yet, so you simply
ride with the man who knows, he assures you, your uncle Jerry.
He drives with one hand on the wheel. His eyes stare at the
street, at you, at the street. His shirt is gray, a color that seems
to mean nothing. You haven't yet learned kidnappings rarely
happen like this, that it isn't strangers your parents should have
worried about. You don't even know what the word *kidnapped*
means, but your parents do. They, like you, are products of their
time, all the TV shows and mass media proclaiming the world
increasingly unsafe, so of course they imagined a man like this,
not the monsters they already know. This is why they've warned

you about strangers and men in vans and children taken from once-safe streets. You will, someday, air on a TV show about missing kids, but you don't know this as you ride slowly out of the neighborhoods you know and into ones you don't, where the houses sit too far apart for screams to be heard, where the basement at a certain home holds ropes and duct tape in one small room, the one that will be yours forever.

**If you take the candy apple:**
You take the candy apple the man offers. It is bright red, and for a moment you think of the poisoned apple the evil witch gives Snow White. Or Sleeping Beauty. Whichever one it is. You do fear, for a moment, that the man wanted to grab your hand as he gave you the apple, but it's a fine fall day and nothing like that has ever happened here, no matter how many TV shows your mother watches or what the nightly news says about abductions.

So the van rolls on and out of your life, you never knowing how close you came to living tied up in a basement, or so your mother would tell you if she knew about the van. She's told you not to eat candy apples because they'll pull the fillings from your teeth and Lord knows she can't afford any more dental work, but she won't be home when you get there because she's at work. Your mother is at work and your father is at work and this is why you walk home alone. Why you sit in an empty house for hours after school. Why they've warned you not to talk to strangers. A therapist could tell you their guilt over leaving you alone has manifested their fear, or that the air around you—in this time, in this place, with the socioeconomic and political upheaval going on, the rise of the twenty-four-hour news network, the changing values brought about by changing technology, a return to what are being called core values, which really means staying afraid of everything outside what we already know—has manifested yours. All you know is that you aren't supposed to take candy from strangers, but at least you weren't stupid enough to get in the van.

So you unlock the front door of your house with the key strung around your neck and put down your bookbag and lock the door behind you and unwrap the bright red shiny candy apple, in which, everyone who grew up in the '80s knows now, there lurks something even shinier, and sharper.

### If you flee:

You've been warned about the man in the van, so you flee through the nearest backyard to the woods behind your house. You cross the small creek, only getting your shoes a little wet. Your mother will be mad about this, she'll worry about a cold, which might turn into pneumonia or the flu or an even worse cold. But you're fleeing the man in the van and so you aren't worried about wet shoes or pneumonia.

You also aren't worried about quicksand, and that's when you hit it. That's always when you hit the things that will hurt you, which is why you have to stay worried all the time. Running full speed from the man in the van, you suddenly sink to your knees. You struggle, but that only makes you sink faster. So you try to slow yourself. You try to remember what the men on TV do when they fall into quicksand, but there is no vine lying close. No tree branch you can use to pull yourself out. No one comes along to help, despite your repeated shouts. You can only wonder if they'll ever find you. You can only think that the men on TV always made it out, but you aren't a man on TV so why didn't your mother warn you? On TV, quicksand is everywhere, every small patch of unknown land holding some goop that will suck you down. The ground, always so steady before, has suddenly become unsettled. Surely your mother would have warned you if she had known what lay in wait in the woods. She would have forbidden you from ever going out there. She has always known how easily young children can be swallowed up by the things their mothers can't foresee, which is why she tries to stay afraid of everything.

**If you ask a neighbor to call the police:**
You sit in the kitchen of the Carlsens, eating cookies, until the policeman arrives. Through the front door you see Mrs. Carlsen talking with the police officer. The police officer wears a big gun and black baton, and he looks at you both kindly and unkindly as he herds you to his car. The man in the van, of course, is long gone.

At home you stand in the front yard while the policeman speaks to your parents. They have come home from work by this time and have been worried, and when the police officer— Officer Clarke—questions you, your mother smokes the cigarettes she's sworn to quit a kabillion times, the ones she calls cancer sticks and coffin nails.

We thought someone had up and taken you, your father says, cracking open his first beer of the night.

We were worried sick, your mother says, inhaling. To Officer Clarke she says, With everything going on in the world . . . she says, if something happened to him . . .

Standing on a fine fall day in the front yard of a street that seems only a little unsafe, you tell Officer Clarke about the man and the van. You tell him about the candy apple he offered and how you thought he was going to grab your arm. You say the van looked sinister, a word you're not sure of but know means something more than scary.

Officer Clarke listens intently, but when you're finished he asks if maybe you're making this up. Was there really a van? he says, and frowns at your emphatic nod. His voice grows a little gruffer when he says, Children can have fun with their imaginations but they mustn't let them get out of hand, and it sounds downright mean when he says, They can't ever lie about men in vans or candy apples. What would happen then? Officer Clarke says. We'd have a whole country seeing bogeymen everywhere, that's what. Everyone would be scared all the time, Officer Clarke says, as he rests one hand on his bright big gun and the other on his black baton, as he looks at your parents and shakes his head as if to say, Where do you think kids come up with such ideas?

**If you ignore the man in the van:**
You ignore the man in the van. You walk home and unlock the door then relock it. You look around the house. It seems still and cold, like the war the news announcers talk about every night on TV, the one that seems to have gotten inside your father, who stays up later now to catch the news again at eleven o'clock, to see what might have changed since he started drinking at six o'clock.

Outside it has begun to rain, a cold light rain that obscures the distance. You wonder how much acid is in the rain. How large the hole in the ozone layer is. You know that the acid in the rain is different from the acid that drug pushers on every street corner try to give children. You have, of course, never seen any drug pushers, but everyone assures you they are out there. Along with men in vans. With quicksand. With razor blades in apples. With nuclear missiles. With every other thing you've been warned about, including the Klingons from *Star Trek* (obviously Russians) and the Stormtroopers from *Star Wars* (obviously Nazis).

The question is then, do you stay at home where it is somewhat safe, if cold and lonely and full of some emotion you can't explain at that age?

**Do you stay there, scared of all the dangers that might possibly exist in the world, or go out?**

**If you go out, do you go out:**
> Now?
> Later?
> At night?
> The next morning?
> Years later?

**If you go out now:**
You're tired of the emotions of that house. Of the sad way your parents come home from work, your mother to the stove and your father to the fridge he keeps in the garage where he used to do woodwork. How your mother's stirring at the stove signals her defeat. How your father sits smoking in his chair, staring at the nightly news but not really seeing it, just listening to the reports of all the bad things out there in the world: the gang-related activity in the city, the drugs and violence; the threat of nuclear war hanging above our heads; the tanking economy, the closing of everything; the AIDS epidemic; the hijackings

and kidnappings in foreign countries, the children found missing or murdered. Your mother is listening as well. Neither of them is talking. Dinner is a quiet affair of tiredness. The house is still cold.

So you unlock the front door and walk out into the world, assuring yourself you'll never become your parents. You'll never take a job you hate just to make ends meet and you'll never fear everything you can't control. You can only try to bring some small light to this world, and it is with this realization, this sudden glow inside you, that you see a brief white light bloom on the horizon and missiles begin to streak skyward, as everyone always said they would.


**If you go out later:**
It's evening, and the lights are coming on in the houses. Cars are coming along the street with their headlamps on and turning into the drives and the blue glow from the TVs are turning the windows to screens. The fine fall day has turned cloudy and cool, but people are still out enjoying the last bit of fall before the real cold sets in or else they are settling themselves in to see what news the day has wrought.

Your parents, too tired from work and the weight they carry with them, choose the TV, but you go out into the evening. Your breath flowers before you. Gone are thoughts of the man in the van, the weight of the world. There is only this moment, you think. A light rain has begun to fall. You can see it slantwise through the streetlights. It rattles on the rooftops of the houses and the world seems fine in its traces until you step out from under the porch and the acid in the rain starts to eat your skin.

**If you go out at night:**

The rain has ended. It is cool after the rain, and the world smells like new hope. You pass the Bixby's house with their pit bull chained in the backyard, the one everyone calls Killer, and the Smith's with their mailbox made to look like a smaller version of their house. At the corner you cut behind the Methodist church with its bell tower that tells you the top of every hour, a reminder that time is passing.

At the park you see the pushers. You wanted to swing for a few minutes, to try to negate the feeling of gravity, of being tied to this time, but the pushers are there, standing just outside the circle of streetlight. They are older than you and scary in the way they wear their hats backward, as if they don't care about convention, so when they wave you over, you go.

In the cooling night they give you a small square of paper, tell you to let it dissolve on your tongue. They say you're only going to take a fun little trip, but for years afterward you don't know who you are. When your parents come to visit you in the institute they can't afford, looking older and older each time, you don't recognize them. You don't recognize anything except the colored lights in your head, the ones that wouldn't be there, you know, sometimes in small moments of clarity, if you hadn't taken anything from the pushers. If you had only listened to all the fears your parents warned you about.

**If you go out the next morning:**

You go to a friend's house to play *Dungeons & Dragons*. It's Saturday and your parents say you should play outside, but you're remembering the man in the van. The apple he offered, like the fruit of knowledge in the Garden of Eden, the one that woke

them up to what the world really was, all its sex and sin and ser-
pents just waiting for the unwary.

So it's inside on Saturday, down in your friend's basement,
making characters who will face the dangerous world for you.
You create a warrior, a big barbarian who would never be afraid
of a man in a van. Kevin creates a cleric and Mark makes a
mage, but some arcane symbol in some ancient dungeon cor-
rupts your characters. Mark's mage flings a fireball at Kevin's
cleric and your warrior cleaves them both as they turn on you,
and you all end up angry at each other.

Saturday ruined, you head home, and somewhere along the
way the anger or the corruption of your character—no one has
ever known how this happened—begins to bother you. It takes a
few weeks, but this anger, this corruption, is like acid. Or quicksand, dragging you down. You can't sit still in Sunday school.
Your teacher asks if you are all right, and you say a word not
found in any scripture, at least not the holy kind.

A year later you're in a Satanic cult, because that's what *Dungeons & Dragons* does to kids in the '80s. It's the same as Ouija
boards. As magic tricks. As witchcraft. So many corrupted children who only wander into the wrong board game.

Soon you're drinking blood. Sacrificing virgins. You become
a man in a white van and abduct children off the streets for your
rituals. Later, you'll murder your own parents, and just before
you kill your mother, she'll say she saw this coming. She'll say
she should have loved you harder.

**If you go out years later:**
But now there are spider eggs in bubble gum. Pop rocks and
soda can erupt inside you and damage your internal organs
(everyone knows that's what happened to Mikey from the Life

cereal commercials). Another Skylab might fall on you because now the stars are clouded with satellites. With missile systems. With Star Wars. You might spontaneously combust. There have been alien abductions, Bigfoot sightings. Killer bees are coming. The hole in the ozone layer now engulfs Antarctica. Other wars have replaced the ones you knew, but no one has yet replaced man's enmity toward those different from him, nor have the men who burn the world stopped burning it, so you go back inside. Stay there, behind the TV screen or the computer screen or the window screen, only occasionally peering out, remembering what it was like out there, once, before everything got inside you. When you have children, try not to transfer your fears to them.

**If you stay home:**
You stay home. You're not sure how, but you know that staying home will keep you safe from the quicksand, the razor blades, the strangers in vans, the nuclear holocaust. From the killer bees, Bigfoot, playing records backward, *D&D*, HIV, AIDS, acid, crack, crystal meth. From rock stars who have swallowed gallons of semen. From alligators in the sewers. From the bathtub and the missing kidney.

What you don't know is how easy it is to fall into patterns of fear. How easy it is to fear everything outside the small rooms of time we walk around in. So you grow old while the world spins on its axis, indifferent. You come to realize the only thing we have to fear is fear itself, but lo, the thing's inside the gate. Your parents will divorce before you turn ten, or twelve, or fourteen. They will grow distant first, as if all their fears have gotten inside them. Or they are tired of being afraid. You'll come to know—years later, worrying for all the things that could happen to your kids—that they had many more fears. The strangers and razors and nuclear war were only the ones on the outside. The drugs and the acid rain were only the ones they could tell you about. They couldn't tell you how hard it was to make ends meet. To struggle through jobs they hated. To worry they weren't enough. That they did not give you enough, didn't love you enough to protect you from everything that might hurt you, including their own faults and failures. They couldn't tell you how much they worried about the world you walked around in, and they couldn't tell you how much they worried they could not change it enough to make it a better place, so they told you in the only way they could.

**The question is: How many of those fears do you carry around now?**

If your answer is none of them, turn back to the beginning. Try again. Don't keep your thumb on the previous page so you can pretend you didn't make a mistake. Try to learn from what you've done, what we've all done, how we've kept our fingers on pages all our lives, always trying to keep the end from coming or wishing we could rewrite it, still somehow unable to understand that never works.

If your answer is all of them, because none of us escape from who we once were, then congratulations. You made it. You're still mostly intact. Now go to the next page, whatever that is.

# Satanic Panic

Sometime in the '70s the Satanists moved in. I'm guessing it was the '70s, that time of crises, both at home and abroad, all of us distracted by *Star Wars* and the possibility of lightsabers, because by the time the '80s rolled around the Satanists were already here, living hidden among us. I knew they were among us because we heard about it all the time, though the details were sketchy, always what someone heard, a friend of a cousin, etc. We didn't know who they were, only that they were out there, somewhere, doing Satan-y things. We heard a lot about sex trafficking and prostitution, heroin and hashish, and something called Satanic ritual abuse, but the truly scary thing, we were told, was that they would keep us from Christ, a fate we would surely regret were it ever to befall us. Christ was the light of our lives, and anything that came between us and that light would ensconce us in darkness.

I'm also assuming now that the Satanists were our collected fears, that in the '80s we believed anyone not God-blessing America was suspect, and we needed some aim to our anger. I know now, because I'm a grown man with Google, that the number of Satanists out there was highly exaggerated and most of the stories were untrue, but at that time we wanted something to hate besides the Soviets, with their missiles and abhorrence of freedom, their insistence in communism and not Christ.

So there weren't really Satanists, not really, but in Middle America in the mid-'80s, with Reagan and the Christian Coalition running the country, we were supposed to say no to drugs and abstain from sex, to abhor AIDS and all the homosexual activities that might lead to contracting it. Satanic ritual abuse, a string of now mostly debunked cases across the US, had our parents terrified. Stranger Danger had them always on the lookout for white vans. There were razors hidden in Halloween candy, and drug pushers handing out acid tabs in the parks. There was crack in the inner cities, the divorce rate was spiraling despite the hard words the men behind the pulpit preached, and the Satanists were behind it all, which made them just as bad as the Soviets. Both wanted to destroy America, the Soviets with their ICBMs, the Satanists with their loud music and sex orgies. Both wanted to keep us from Christ, which meant we had to be constantly on the lookout, not only for communists but for pentagrams drawn on playgrounds, for drugs and sex parties, for songs that, wound backward, told us to worship the evil one, to murder our parents and play *Dungeons & Dragons*, a game that, like the Ouija board, let the demons in.

The first suspect was a boy I'll call Billy, who only the year before had entered a program for drug rehabilitation, who, rumor had it, smoked weed outside the shop class, who wore his hair long and (supposedly) had several tattoos at the ripe age of fourteen.

This was late '83 or '84, although it's hard to remember across so many times and tides, sometime around when the world came close to ending itself, the two biggest boys on the block installing radars and computers to track the missiles we feared would be flying, everyone watching *The Road Warrior,*

*Blade Runner, The Terminator,* which told us the world would eventually end unless we could go back in time.

As the story goes, Billy saw a bonfire in the woods. He crept up on it and there they were, dark shadowy figures dancing or drinking blood or fornicating under a full moon. We should have known Billy was full of shit, and when he disappeared a few weeks later we should have known he had, once again, been sent somewhere for his weed addiction, his parents being of the belief that one could become addicted to weed.

But Billy didn't show up to school one day, and the rumors ran everywhere: Billy had been abducted. He had been killed in ritual sacrifice. He was seen wearing a goat's head. He was drinking the blood of virgins.

These types of stories were circulating all over the country. The Church of Satan had formed in the late '60s. Books like *The Satanic Bible,* published in 1969, became seminal texts for modern Satanism. The movie *The Exorcist* (1973) showed us what would happen if kids played with the occult.

Suddenly we were seeing Satanists everywhere. In 1983 allegations against a child day care center claimed that the workers sexually abused the children, that the workers could fly, and that children were taken into secret tunnels to be abused. Police in the '80s distributed documents to help teachers and school administrators pick out students who were into Satanism and the occult. At my small Arkansas school, several kids were accused of making the "horned hand"—a symbol by which occult members identified themselves—in a school photo.

So Billy's story was nothing new. There were stories all over school—pentagrams supposedly drawn on church steps, a nativity scene vandalized, the baby Jesus's head cut off. Hunters found dead deer in the woods, no source of death, but strange symbols carved into trees or circles where no vegetation would grow.

Girls who wore dark eyeliner were whispered about. Anyone who listened to Judas Priest or Black Sabbath needed to come to know Jesus. It occurs to me that of course conservatives attacked the way we looked and the way we dressed and the music we listened to; they were scared of a changing world, one they feared could end at any time, and religion has always been a panacea for such people, a way to assure themselves they'll continue, even if the world does not.

Another kid named Nick said he heard strange noises in the woods at night near his house. He had seen fires as well, only these were never in the same spot and seemed to move, or maybe there were many of them. Nick didn't know, but he gathered quite a crowd telling about it, the way ninth graders gathered a crowd when they made up some story about having sex, emphasizing words like *swallowed.*

One night Nick's sliding glass door supposedly blew inward, though there was not a tornado or straight-line wind strong enough to shatter glass anywhere in the area. I assume now that Nick had done it, either accidentally or on purpose, probably to hide some greater sin, like maybe his dog had shit on the floor, or maybe he made the whole thing up, but by this time we no longer cared about Nick's stories. By this time we knew a real Satanist, one who had lived in the evil city of San Francisco, who had shot up and snorted and smoked and drank and sexed and sinned and led secret rites and rituals. In short, a man who had done everything we weren't supposed to, and everything real Satanists did.

I first heard of Mike Warnke at church. I was attending the Baptist church just down the road, where we prayed to Jesus and promised to stay away from anything that might keep us from Him.

Warnke was a former Satanist turned born-again Christian. He was the kind of man Christians loved to hear speak. At our small rural church, no one ever did anything to repent against except maybe masturbation, my major crime, one I pursued with a zeal I never had for religion. But Christians love to hear how badly people have fucked up their lives before finding Jesus. They love the stories of alcoholics and drug users, the gamblers and gays who have since reverted to straight men.

Warnke self-identified as a Christian comedian, which sounded like saying snowmobile whisperer, or knife eater— I knew what the words meant, but they didn't make any sense together. The Christians I knew weren't funny. They were always preparing for the end. I don't mean they were doomsday preppers, like the people you occasionally see on TV learning how to salt meat or dig an underground bomb shelter. They were, instead, always certain Jesus was Coming Back. They used capital letters, too, as if it were an event and they had front-row tickets. The Rapture would come, and how joyful we would be, and even at twelve I knew there was something supremely fucked up about looking forward to Armageddon.

Warnke used humor to lead kids to Christ. He also used his stories of Satanism. I was too young to know the wonderful pleasures of drugs. He said he was addicted to heroin, that he had scabs all over his body from shooting crystal, but I only knew that drugs were bad. When he said he had women who worshipped him almost as much as they worshipped Satan, I imagined mirrors and goblets and lurid light. I wasn't quite sure of the logistics of lovemaking, but I knew it wouldn't be something anyone wanted to watch. (I had not yet heard of porn, so I did not know that lots of people wanted to watch sex.)

According to Warnke, at some point he was introduced to Satanism. I say "some point" because even Warnke's own accounts vary. My friends and I were passing recorded cassette tapes back and forth during Sunday school and listening to them at night, when the cool kids were listening to Mötley Crüe shout at the devil. Warnke started slowly, telling a few jokes before getting into the stuff we wanted to hear, because kids are drawn to all the dark places in the world, as anyone who's ever read *Where the Wild Things Are* will tell you.

After his parents died, Warnke ended up in California, living with family. By all accounts he was a normal high school kid. It was in college where the trouble began. First, he started drinking so much he couldn't pay attention in class. He was hungover any time he wasn't drunk, and his stomach hurt from all the drinking.

Another student introduced Mike to weed, and he started smoking it, mostly because of his upset stomach. But, as any Christian counselor will tell you, weed is a gateway drug, and Warnke went on to harder stuff—peyote first, then pills. He volunteered for a study on LSD, and then he got into the hard stuff.

On his *Mike Warnke Alive!* album, Warnke says:

I'd had hepatitis four times from shooting up with dirty needles. I had scabs all over my face from shooting up crystal. I was a speed freak. I weighed 110 pounds soaking wet. My skin had turned yellow. My hair was falling out. My teeth were rotting out of my head. I'd been pistol-whipped five or six times. My jaw had been broken. My nose had been almost ripped off. I had a bullet hole in my right leg. Two bullet holes in my left leg.

The man who introduced him to weed, named Dean Armstrong in *The Satan Seller,* Warnke's 1972 memoir, was also a Satanist, and he decided it was time for Mike to be initiated into the cult. At Black Mass in an orange grove, Warnke, black-robed, incanting blasphemy while a naked woman lay on an altar, listened to others offer their souls to Satan. He signed his name in blood and, later, took over the coven by killing a cat and drawing an upside-down star on a naked girl's stomach, which caused a demon to speak from her mouth.

As a Satanist priest, Warnke had lots of sex. Orgies, but also the "soft, pink kind," as he describes it. Two women came with the apartment he was given, sex slaves who wanted him as much as he wanted drugs. The rituals grew more degenerate, from killing cats to the rape of a woman, a rape Warnke did not participate in but rather watched, ravenous. He also flew to various cities, recruiting for Satan and, apparently, buying drugs.

But Warnke crumpled under the strain of too many responsibilities and too many drugs. He was intentionally overdosed by one of the sex slaves and dropped off at the nearest emergency room. After drying out, Warnke joined the navy to get away from the Satanists, and while he was in boot camp, he met two Christians who converted him.

It's a fascinating story. The problem is, very little of it seems to have actually happened. In 1992 Warnke was exposed by the Christian magazine *Cornerstone,* the same magazine that had debunked Lauren Stratford's *Satan's Underground* the year before. There were major inconsistencies in Warnke's story, including but not limited to his claim that Charles Manson had attended one of the Satanic rituals. The friends he describes in the book have contradicted his accounts. Pictures taken during the time dispute his descriptions of himself as emaciated with yellow skin and scabs on his face. He wasn't a high priest.

He didn't sacrifice virgins or drink their blood or do anything that a Satanist is supposed to do. By all accounts he went to college. He might have messed around once or twice with a Ouija board, but no Satanism, no sex, no snorting or shooting, no ritual sacrifice. He went to classes. He went to the coffeeshop. After one semester, he enlisted in the navy, where he converted to Christianity.

The obvious answer as to why Warnke lied is money. But I also keep coming back to how badly we wanted to believe him. *The Satan Seller* was an instant bestseller among the religious community and has sold over three million copies since its release. Warnke's comedy has sold over a million records, and his shows and ministry certainly paid well.

Many of the Satanist "memoirs" of the early '70s have now been debunked, but the Satanic Panic still won't die. During the 2016 election, Hillary Clinton was accused of running a child sex-trafficking ring from the basement of a pizza place that did not have a basement. Yet the story went viral. QAnon conspiracy theorists claimed Trump was waging a secret war against a deep state of Democratic elites and Hollywood stars who were pedophiles and Satan worshippers, all of this proving that some people will believe any bullshit as long as it fits into their suspicions or promotes whatever panic they're already indulging in. The 2016 North Carolina "Bathroom Bill" is one example, a law that was supposedly passed to protect the straights, as George Carlin called them, from the predations of trans men or women.

The problem is these predations are myths. But trans people themselves are attacked often, as thousands of recorded cases show. They are much more likely to be attacked, beaten, murdered, or raped, and they are more likely to die by suicide, but the law was passed to protect others from them because people had "heard stories."

It's hard to understand why we wanted to believe so badly that Satanists were out there. I know Christianity was losing support. I know the divorce rate was skyrocketing and people were leaving the church and church leaders proclaimed we were losing our way. I don't know about that last part, but congregations certainly lost millions of dollars trying to find our way back.

I know we were so scared of the Soviets that perhaps even Satan seemed a lesser evil. I think now we were so worried about missiles that we saw monsters everywhere, so scared of what we couldn't see that we decided everything we saw was dangerous.

I went to see Warnke in 1984 or '85. I don't remember the year, but I know it was before I started driving, before I learned about the wonders of alcohol or tasted the sins of the flesh. I had joined a Baptist church youth group, which operated, like all church youth groups, on the idea that teens are constantly looking to get into trouble, that, left alone, teenagers will drink and do drugs, fight and fornicate and fuck up their lives so badly that in twenty years, when they come back to Christ, they'll be an inspiration to the rest of the church. But in the meantime, they might end up dead or in jail, which is infinitely worse in a small Southern town, and therefore they need to be guided, idle hands being the devil's workshop or whatever.

So every Saturday night was movie night. We would all pile into the youth room and arrange ourselves on the floor and watch some annoyingly wholesome movie in which two Christians stay Christ-y the entire time. We stuffed ourselves with popcorn and peanuts and candy bars, not caring about our acne, though we might pray that God not let our zits get too big. We were always praying, either for everyone to have a safe trip home or to sleep well or to resist Satan in the form of impure thoughts. We prayed before and after every youth group, and we were advised to pray every morning and every night, to constantly be praying so we might keep away the sinful world. I should clarify that when they spoke of the sinful world, they meant we had to watch out not only for the kidnappings and cults but also that, out there, outside the church, there were thoughts that could keep us from God, which, of course, makes me wonder how much they really believed in God if sin was so strong that even catching a whiff of it could send us careening down a path that led to killing kittens with a curved knife.

When we rode the church bus anywhere—to high school basketball games or football games or to see Mike Warnke—Sherry B., the preacher's wife, would every so often ask for a show of hands. She wasn't asking us to vote but rather to raise our hands in the air to prove we weren't touching one another inappropriately. I don't know if she believed there was a lot of fingerbanging going on, or handys or head there in the dark of the bus, but I do remember it worked as a constant reminder of our sexuality. It was hard enough to sit by Jocelyn Stokes and smell the shampoo and moisturizer she used on her skin; it was even harder to be constantly reminded I wasn't supposed to touch her.

This seems a point where I should say something about abstinence, how if we walk around pretending desire doesn't exist, we often end up more desirous. Being constantly reminded I wasn't supposed to touch Jocelyn made me want to put my hands all over her, a thing I eventually did, and a thing that was exactly as awesome as I thought it would be, considering how much Sherry B. thought I shouldn't do it. And that's a lesson I learned early—that if they don't want you to do it, it's probably awesome, because the thing they learned is that all the awesome things are dangerous and should be avoided at all costs.

In the purview of the church, sex or drugs or alcohol are all slippery slopes. Holding hands on the church bus, quite obviously, leads to anal sex. Smoking pot leads to heroin, and heroin leads to Satan.

No one ever said these things out loud. It was implied. It was implicit in the Bible lessons we learned, in the raising of our hands to show we weren't rubbing genitals during the wholesome movies we watched. Besides the basketball games and movie nights, we had scavenger hunts, board games, and Bible study groups. We went to church camp for a week each summer, sitting in the Arkansas heat and talking about hell. We played putt-putt, went to swimming pools and, most often, other churches, either for more Bible study or to listen to their shitty choir, which sounded a lot like our shitty choir, all of it designed to keep us from the things out in the world that would derail our daily walk with Christ.

Mike Warnke was speaking at Van Buren Baptist Church in Van Buren, Arkansas. We rode the old white bus with Sherry B. shouting every few minutes for us to show our hands. I sat beside Jocelyn, thinking about what my hands could be doing if they weren't constantly being called upon to prove their innocence. In the parking lot were dozens of other busses, kids streaming inside with the same dazed look on their faces as on ours, as if they had just missed an opportunity for entanglement and were now regretting this whole ordeal but also already thinking about the trip home, when maybe their version of Sherry B. would fall asleep and some action could occur.

When we went in, the organist was softly playing "Onward Christian Soldiers" on the large pipe organ that soared above the sacristy. It was a large church, not one of the megachurches like that asshole Joel Osteen has down in Houston, but enough seats for a few hundred, all of them full of kids with their eyes closed and hands up and heads back, swaying a little to the music as they prepared for Mike.

Warnke was not the first traveling preacher we'd seen. Occasionally missionaries came to our church, usually men who had gone to Ghana or the Philippines or some other distant, near-the-equator country. They always wore the same hot-weather suits, which weren't suits at all but thin dress shirts embroidered as if to make up for being short sleeved. These men always spoke in a soft monotone, as if the foreign lands they'd visited required a different approach, one that involved fewer stories of sin and more of sacrifice. Their wives were often called up to tell us about the women they had testified to, and this always ended with a lesson on what they, the white women, learned, their general expression being one of shock that women with nonwhite skin could teach them something about life and love. Sometimes their children testified as well, short, torturous speeches about what they had learned—God is everywhere, God loves everyone, even those without long pants—and these missionaries always ended their speeches with the number of converts they had counted.

It was also around this time I learned of the term *missionary sex,* so named because Christian missionaries to foreign countries spoke against the evils of doggy style, or woman-on-top, or maybe, if they knew the term, reverse cowgirl. They wanted their converts to engage only in missionary-style sex: man on top, woman's legs spread, doors locked, lights out. And it occurred to me that Christians wanted to control even the position in which people fucked, as if they needed to make it as procreative and prescriptive as possible.

We also had tent revivals in my small Southern town. Southside Baptist Church put up a big tent in their parking lot every fall and would bring in an itinerant preacher, usually a man who'd gained some small fame either as a local televangelist or as someone who had fallen prey to Satan in his past and now was here to warn us of the dangers. These revivals went on for a week. Some nights people stood and confessed their crimes—alcohol, drugs, and sex were always at the top of the list, but there were also gamblers and embezzlers and women who gave up their kids for adoption. Other nights the stories were of affirmation—how God gave them sustenance when they were hungry, how He looked out for them when they were sick. A woman who lost her child to cancer would stand and say she had come to understand it was God's will, and a woman whose child had been cured would praise the Lord for this gift. Apparently, if we survive whatever circumstances surround us, it is God's will. If we do not, well, then, God has mysterious ways.

At church camp, the sermons were not so much about God's mysterious ways but about Satan's deceptive ones. Satan was always out there, and he was always looking for us to slip up. One preacher whose name I no longer remember spent an entire sermon on Christian rock music. His belief was that there was no such thing, no matter what the song lyrics said, no matter how many of the band members had been saved. He kept saying Christian rock was the same as Christian pornography, a statement that garnered a lot of concern from the overseers of the camp and a lot of interest from the teenagers, since we were just learning about porn ourselves, stealing *Playboy* magazines from our stepfathers and renting R-rated movies that might show a boob. If there was such a thing as Christian pornography, we realized, we could watch it without all that guilt they tried to lay on us.

Speaking of guilt, my fifth-grade teacher told us that dressing up on Halloween was evil, because once you put on the skin of a witch or warlock, demons could get inside you. I would say she was an outlier, as she went to the weird church that wouldn't let women wear makeup or pants, but this was also a town in which the school principal read the Bible verse of the day over the loudspeaker every morning and the Lord's Prayer before every football game, so maybe she was as mainstream as any of us.

This is the same school that, a few years later, brought in a man named David Toma, who was not a preacher but a former cop. I bring him up now because he had the same effect on our small town as an evangelist. Toma had been a narcotics cop with a 98 percent conviction rate. He had cleared thousands of kilos of smack off the street, whatever the fuck smack was.

He stood on our gymnasium floor and told us about the dangers of drugs. He told us about the pimps and prostitutes, young men and women who got caught up in the cold world of drugs and couldn't find their way out. He told us about murders committed over a single line of coke. He spoke of men high on meth who stayed awake for weeks, until they hallucinated angels and demons. He spoke of men who had blown their minds out and were now nothing more than a shell, and he ended with the woman who, tripping on LSD, had cooked her baby daughter like a turkey—Toma had entered the apartment just as she was sitting down to eat.

I later learned this last one is an urban legend, which, in my mind, makes Toma just as fake as Warnke, but our teachers ate it up. Most of the students did too. The seniors started a group where anyone could come talk to them about drug use. There were people crying in the aisles, confessing that they had stolen some cigarettes and smoked, sure now that those few drags meant they were destined for heavier drugs—and perhaps baby cooking. That night Toma gave another talk to the adults in the town, this one even more explicit than the one he gave us. He told them every one of their children would try drugs unless they stopped them, and for weeks the town seemed transformed. Nancy Reagan was blathering on about "just saying 'no,'" and now the townspeople were driving around drunk, on the lookout for drugs.

Toma ended with resources and hotlines, and a crowd of people went down to talk to him. It was not that different from church, where every sermon ended with the invitation, which is when the piano plays softly and the preacher asks for anyone who has not been living right to come accept Jesus Christ as their personal savior. During every revival a flood of kids would come forward, crying. There was something wrong with them, they said, and they wanted it fixed. The counselors or preachers assured them that Jesus would fix it, and so they walked away believing they were saved from their own sins. At church camp every year, a few people would trickle down on Tuesday and Wednesday, but Thursday night, before we went home on Friday, the trickle became a flood. Dozens, then perhaps hundreds, of teenagers sweating in the Arkansas heat would swear their lives to Christ, and it occurs to me, recalling all this, how the ceiling fans swayed, how we swayed along to the soft organ music rolling out into the summer night, how we looked inside and saw all the ways they told us we were flawed. How scared we were, standing there, hoping there was something that could save us.

When Warnke came out on stage, we didn't know if we were supposed to be scared or not. We knew Warnke was a comedian, that he had been a Satanist drug dealer, but we weren't prepared for how he looked. He was wearing something that looked more like a jumpsuit than a church suit, hair long, overweight, voice high pitched and breathy. He looked like a guy who worked at a grocery store. But he said there wasn't just one kind of Christian, that there was room enough for everyone, and—looking at his saggy jumpsuit and hair we would have called un-Christian—we knew he must be right if the church leaders had allowed him to be there.

Warnke employed a narrative style of comedy. He told stories about his alcoholic parents. About growing up at a truck stop and learning to cuss from truckers. About Catholic foster parents and parochial school. Warnke claims to be a storyteller, not a preacher, but he does offer—on his 1976 album anyway, and when I heard him in 1984—sympathy. Understanding. He's warm and compassionate. He speaks of God's forgiveness.

He also speaks of his time as a Satanist, though in *Alive*, his first album, he skips over most of it. *The Satan Seller* had been out for four years at that point, so maybe he figured everyone had read it, and maybe he was sure everyone had read it by 1984 when I saw him. On the album, he does say he spent seven years as a Satanist priest, that he dealt drugs and took drugs, but he doesn't want to give the gory details. He says he doesn't have to roll up his sleeves so the audience can see the scars on his forearms from shooting up. He doesn't have time, Warnke says, to talk about chopping people's fingers off, because he's too busy testifying for the Lord.

When Warnke gave the invitation at the end, he did not ask everyone to close their eyes. He said he did not want Satan to be able to say that people only came down to the front because all eyes were closed. He said if you wanted to give your life to Jesus, you should do it in front of everyone. That it was a lifetime commitment. And look, I was as scared as everyone around me. I went down to the front, the same as I had several times, trying to find something that would wash away the fear I often felt. I shook Mike Warnke's hand. He hugged me there on the stage. If you would have told me he was a fraud, I wouldn't have cared, just like so many people believe the televangelists are good Christians, even as they ask for more money. Those who are alone don't care, because for a little bit they feel less alone, less afraid. The Satanic Panic happened because Christians were scared. Because we were all scared.

We still are. Of terrorist attacks. Of terminal illness, for ourselves or our loved ones. Of identity theft. Climate change. School shootings, government corruption, people who look different from us.

After Warnke left the stage, we filed out into the night. I'd like to say I felt different, but Sherry B. closed her eyes on the bus ride home, and I touched Jocelyn in several inappropriate places. Later that night, at home in bed, when heat lightning began flashing on the far horizon and I thought for a moment it might be nuclear missiles, I wondered what we were so scared of. Or, rather, why we were always scared: of men and their missiles, of Satan and his minions, of drugs and sex and strangers in white vans. There was a fear for everything we saw, some story circulating around, like the kid supposedly decapitated on a roller coaster.

It was like we couldn't put it down, the fear. Like it had gotten inside us. We were as addicted as any drug user. We wanted these fears because they made us feel something besides the constant exhaustion of living near the end times. The end times were coming, we were told, but add some silly story about how swallowed gum stays with you for seven years and one can almost laugh at how absurd earth's imminent destruction sounds.

So we keep pledging to be better, either giving our lives to religion or starting some new program that will make everything okay. We quit drinking. We lose weight. We get up early to run in the morning. But we never feel safer, and we never change the problems of the world.

Eventually I drifted away from the church. Eventually the Cold War ended, and the Satanic Panic faded away. I went to college and got married and had children and told my daughters stories that made the sermons of my youth seem as distant as hell. I did not tell them there was a fiery pit waiting beneath their feet, but I did warn them about strangers, so maybe I'm the same as the men who would have us afraid all the time.

I read about Warnke's discrediting sometime in the 2000s. I had forgotten all about him. I hadn't been to church in twenty years, had begun to believe that all religion was just a wondering about what was out there, an attempt to understand why man is so small standing under the stars.

But I was suddenly struck numb as I thought of Warnke, as I remembered youth group. The smell of Jocelyn Stokes. The rhythm and hum of that old church bus rattling down the highway. When I listened to Warnke's first album on YouTube, I remembered every word. Every single word of it, and I sat remembering for a long time after it ended: the night we drove to hear him speak, the headlights of passing cars lighting Jocelyn's face for a moment, how serious she looked when I took her hand; the all-night event one cool fall weekend in 1983, none of us knowing how close we had come, in September, to war with the Soviet Union. I remembered the scavenger hunts, the basketball games, the movie nights. Sitting in the back of church with Casey Thomas and Sean Rowe, making fart noises with our hands in our armpits. Singing in the choir, how our voices rebounded to the heavens and back. We still sounded like shit, but singing was one pure small joy in a world that didn't want to hear teenage voices.

What I keep coming back to was how much fun we had when no one told us we weren't supposed to be having fun. How unscared we were when no one told us to be scared. It was only when they told us to be scared that we were scared. It was when they reminded us of sin that we remembered to be on the lookout for Satan. That holding hands might lead to sex and sex might lead to sin and sin might lead to our eternal suffering. That not only was Satan out there but the Soviets were too. That their missiles were aimed at us, as Reagan kept reminding us, so we had to aim ours at them, and so it went, sad spirals of fear all the way down.

It's only now I realize it wasn't really the Soviets or Satan we were afraid of—it was the darkness inside us. We knew we were flawed. That's one thing religion gets right—we are, all of us, flawed, driven by our desires or envy, always wanting the world when we can't even take care of ourselves.

Too many church leaders believed the end was coming. That God's forgiveness was a gift, but only after Armageddon. Only after the Four Horsemen had come and the Antichrist had risen and Satan, whom weird Mike Warnke said he'd worshipped before turning to God, had been resealed in his eternal hell would we reap the rewards of following Christ.

So we didn't think there would be a future. We went around scared of both the sky and the earth. We couldn't see past what was happening right before us, the changing shape of what we knew, so we never fought for a better future. We had begun to realize how small and insignificant we were, how easily everything could end. We knew the world was much larger than the small towns we lived in, that everything outside our purview was terrifying because we couldn't control it, which was why so many tried to so hard. Old Satan was out there, and we had to always be on the lookout, only we had begun to suspect there was no Satan, just ourselves and our small sad way of seeing the world.

# Star Wars

My first real memory may very well be the opening scene from *Star Wars: A New Hope,* in which, after the floating text tells us the world is at war, Darth Vader and his stormtroopers seize Princess Leia's ship. While rebel soldiers line the hallways, stormtroopers blast open the air-locked door and begin firing lasers. A moment later, Vader comes through with his black mask and heavy breath, cape sweeping the ground behind him, and sometime after that we see lightsabers and landspeeders, X-wing and TIE fighters, the *Millennium Falcon* and the Death Star, and I'll say now that *ignite* is too weak a word to describe what that movie did to my imagination.

Suddenly we were all looking at the stars, wondering what went on above our heads. Or we were arguing if lightsabers were real, if we could learn to use the force to move things with our minds or convince our mothers to take us swimming. I still wonder, occasionally, when I've left a light on after climbing into bed, if I couldn't just turn it off with a wave of my hand.

The second word in the movie title is *wars,* and we played at them constantly. At Christmas, cardboard wrapping paper tubes turned into lightsabers. My mother's station wagon morphed into the *Millennium Falcon,* and any truck following too closely was a TIE fighter. On summer nights, lightning strikes might have been a battle above us, thunder the crash of star destroyers or Death Stars.

We also collected all the characters. My brother and I pooled our allowances to buy the action figures then set them up against one another on the floor of our room. Stormtroopers murdered Jawas. Sand People rose from the rocks and struck Luke Skywalker. Han Solo shot Greedo, and Obi-Wan chopped off that walrus-guy's arm before being killed in the end by Vader. We made them fight until we grew afraid. Alderaan got annihilated. The Death Star was destroyed.

It seems there was so much to be scared of in the late '70s. Bombs fell constantly at nearby Fort Chaffee, as if the army were gearing up for war, and in 1979 the Soviet Union invaded Afghanistan. In September of the same year, the US discovered a Soviet combat brigade in Cuba and refused to ratify the SALT II treaty, which would have limited the number of nuclear missiles on both sides of the world. I heard only the rumblings of war then, looking as I was to the skies, but when the bombs from Chaffee struck, I could feel the impact beneath the soles of my shoes.

The year after the Soviet invasion of Afghanistan, *The Empire Strikes Back* came out. Critics claim it the best film in the series, but I left the theater sick to my stomach. Han Solo was taken captive by Boba Fett after being betrayed by Lando Calrissian, who was in turn choked by Chewbacca. Luke lost his hand, and worse still, we learned Vader was his father. The whole galaxy, it seemed, was collapsing.

By the time *Return of the Jedi* was released in 1983, the world was close to war. In September, not long after the movie premiered, a Soviet Su-15 shot down a Korean airliner with an American congressman on board. Less than a month later, a Soviet early warning system falsely detected the launch of

American Minutemen missiles, and the world hovered on the edge of annihilating itself. Some of us were still watching the skies, worried that what we saw on the movie screen might not be make-believe.

That same year—I was eleven, my voice close to dropping into the lower tones of a man—President Reagan announced his Strategic Defense Initiative. To save the United States from the evils of the Soviet Union, we would put lasers and interceptors in space to shoot down Soviet missiles in case of a nuclear attack. Because of its reliance on futuristic technologies like lasers, subatomic particle beams, and electromagnetic rail guns, the SDI was nicknamed "Star Wars," although the animation on our TV screens showing how it would work was much less realistic than any movie.

I don't know if we grew older and forgot childish games because the real world colored our view of the movies, but shortly after Reagan's announcement on national television, my brother and I burned all our *Star Wars* figures. We lined them up on a rock wall behind our house and held a lighter to a can of hair spray, creating a flamethrower. We watched their faces melt, the same way TV shows such as *The Day After* assured us we would melt when the missiles flew and the warheads landed after the lasers in space failed to stop them. Perhaps we knew then that despite the opening line "a long time ago in a galaxy far, far away," here was our future: men like the ones we would someday become building missiles and lasers and lightsabers and Death Stars until all the universe was destroyed.

In the seventh *Star Wars* movie, *The Force Awakens,* a new war begins. A weapon even more powerful than the Death Star, with the ability to destroy five planets, has been built, and a small band of rebels must destroy it. Some critics have complained the movie is simply a reiteration of the other ones: the same threats, the same weapons, the same heroes, and it's hard not to argue that history repeats itself, even in movies.

At the end of *Rogue One,* the eighth movie released in the *Star Wars* franchise, everyone dies. The Death Star fires from the skies, and a massive tsunami washes over the rebels. Two of the main characters sit on the beach in the last sunset of their lives. A moment later, time loops around, and again Vader invades the rebel ship. The movie ends where my childhood began: the world is at war, Vader is breathing heavily in his black mask, and there's only a tiny sliver of hope that the evil Galactic Empire will ever be defeated, that men will ever stop attacking one another.

In the *Star Wars* universe, the cost of using the force was the evil that overcame the wielder if he used it in anger. The only limit was what he could imagine, and I wonder now how much war we can imagine, how much all our warring will cost us. I wonder how we would use the force today, if we would choke all the enemies who came at us, if we would destroy the Death Stars we've already put in space.

In our world, what we call the real world, forgetting how art imitates life, the sky is full of interceptor missiles, the descendants of Reagan's Star Wars program. The United States has invaded Afghanistan; we've been there longer than the Soviets ever were. The old Soviet Union no longer exists, but there's evidence Russia hacked the 2016 election, that they've engaged in a new kind of war in addition to the one they started in Ukraine. In 2019 Trump announced an initiative to build a state-of-the-art missile defense system to combat what he feared might fall on us out of the sky. Along with the initiative to put missiles among the stars, he also announced a Space Force, modeled after the Marine Corps, which included changes to the Air Force to bolster national space security. This outer space security concern stems from the fear Russia might get there before us, which makes me think of Reagan and my *Star Wars* figures, how my brother and I burned our little green army men first, then turned our attention to the stars.

Forty years later we're still turning our attention to the stars, wondering what might fall on us, if there's any way to protect ourselves from ourselves. All this reminds me I'm still afraid of the same things I was afraid of as a child. Some days I think the movies are real and we're watching the last hour of humanity. You'll have to decide if there's any hope.

# Left Turn at Albuquerque

In the late '70s, around the time President Carter was negotiating the SALT II treaty with the Soviet Union, my parents' marriage began to fall apart. My father had taken a job out of town, and my mother suspected not all his nights away were work related. There were often shouting matches and slamming doors. My mother smoked on the porch when my father left, smoke curling around her long brown hair; when he came home, mustache neatly trimmed for his new white-collar job, she ashed out her cigarette and went inside before he could talk to her. At night we watched *Dallas* and *Knots Landing* in silence. Someone was always leaving or on the verge of leaving, and to escape the acrimony that had crept into all the comings and goings, I hid in my room with pencil and paper in front of me and tried to draw out the incessant anger.

Our first-grade teacher had recently announced an art contest, and I decided, in the way only a six-year-old could, that winning it might save my parents' marriage. I don't remember what the prize was, but I imagined it being awarded to me in front of the school, with friends and neighbors and visiting dignitaries in attendance. My parents would look tenderly on what they had created together and then reconcile their previously irreconcilable differences.

What I knew of art at the time came from Bugs Bunny cartoons. I spent what seems now weeks working on my drawing. Holed up in my room while my parents either fought or moved around one another like furniture, I wore out sheet after sheet of first expensive art paper, and then, after my mother saw my tortured lines, plain notebook paper. The contest specified we were to draw characters from a book that had influenced us, and the other kids in my class were sketching cats in hats and Horton hearing Whos and Max the Terrible and the Wild Things, who roared their terrible roars and gnashed their terrible teeth.

I had never read a book about any of the *Looney Tunes* characters, but when asked what art influenced me as a six-year-old, I envisioned the bull charging and Bugs jerking the flag away, an anvil hidden behind it. Or Bugs lowering the drawbridge on Yosemite Sam's head, forcing the flattened Sam to ask that Bugs close it up again. While my parents tried to keep their voices down on Saturday mornings, my brother and I sat in front of the TV, waiting for *The Bugs Bunny/Road Runner Hour*. Sylvester chased Tweety, who was in turn chased by Granny with a broom. Wile E. Coyote waited for the Road Runner but found himself running from his own diabolical devices. Yosemite Sam or Elmer Fudd or the two hillbilly brothers hunted Bugs, but instead of fleeing he turned their own schemes against them.

Not only was I certain of my superior artistic skills, I was also certain the others had chosen the wrong characters to draw. I loved Max and the Wild Things and wanted to sail in and out of weeks and over a year when my parents were too busy flinging words at one another to cook dinner, or when the house grew cold because no one built a fire. I loved Narnia, the secret world a child could access simply by sweeping past the old coats in a wardrobe, and I loved the bridge to Terabithia one could swing across over the swollen stream, but Bugs Bunny never needed to escape to another land, unless one counts Albuquerque.

What I didn't know was that I could not draw. After my futile attempts at original art, I traced my entry from a picture. Even my tracing skills were horrible. Other students had used water-colors and art pencils, and I was disappointed in my notebook paper and No. 2 pencil. When time came to turn in our draw-ings, I hid mine in my desk.

My first interests in history and classical music and space flight came from the cartoons. In foreign countries and castles and cannons, in ships and sword fights. When every nightly news program broadcast our deteriorating relations with the Soviets and every Saturday morning meant a fight in our cold house, my brother and I turned to cartoons to escape the fears we felt, either from our parents or the end of the world.

The South as depicted in the cartoons was most often a gen-teel, caricatured version far removed from rural Arkansas in the late '70s. We lived in a small community outside a small town in a small area of a small state. My father was always searching for better work, and my mother wanted to go back to school, meaning neither of them was happy with where we were. The only building close to us was a church, which felt as stifling and constricting as the area in which we lived.

Even the time was depressing, in the way only childhood can be. I didn't know then about the hijackings and kidnap-pings in foreign countries, but I could feel the fear that per-vaded ours. I didn't know about President Carter and the SALT II treaty, nor did I know about the Russian invasion of Afghani-stan. I was only vaguely aware that an actor was sure to be our next president—a man who once looked young but seemed, to many, on the verge of a new decade, to be old and doddering—or that in our corner of the country we were becoming more conservative.

My brother and I felt only the rumblings of the times, like storms in the distance that were still far enough away to be of no worry, for now. The arguments between my mother and father were real enough, but terrorists and Soviet missiles, if we even knew what the words meant, were less real than cartoons. The news my father watched was peripheral, something we could ignore, like the anger in our house, when Bugs came on. He never faced a foe he couldn't defeat in less than eight minutes, and it was easier for me to believe in spaceships than airplanes being hijacked or missiles crossing an ocean. It was easier to believe a rabbit and a speech-impeded hunter knew the words to Wagner's "Ride of the Valkyries" than to reflect on the depression lingering in our house.

I found hope in the way Bugs overcame adversity. Yosemite Sam had pistols and anger. Elmer Fudd had a rifle, or a spear and magic helmet. Marvin the Martian had the Illudium PU-36 Explosive Space Modulator, and ten thousand instant Martians—just add water. Bugs's ability to defeat his foes was born of ingenuity and daring, two traits I seemed to lack. I saw myself as an ineffectual child, one of the random animals fleeing from the Tasmanian Devil. My two main states were sad or guilty, depending on the circumstance. I was sad I couldn't draw and guilty about the starving kids in Africa who had begun to appear on our TV between commercials for toys and cereal. I felt guilty when I received a gift I didn't like or when my mother bought me clothes I knew I would never wear, and I felt both sad and guilty when she sat on the porch and smoked in the last light after a fight with my father.

I was never sad watching cartoons. The format precludes it. Even when a character dies, he doesn't die. Sylvester floats toward heaven playing a harp, white wings attached to his back. Wile E. Coyote blows himself up a hundred times and plunges from the cliff a hundred more. Daffy Duck shoots his own face off and reattaches it. The only war was of the personal kind, a feud that everyone knew always existed and always would: Sylvester versus Tweety, the Road Runner versus Wile E. Coyote, Bugs versus Yosemite or Elmer or Daffy.

In the first grade, I was often at war, though I never extricated myself from the circumstances the way Bugs did. I was small, and my anger at my parents' impending divorce often landed me in fist fights, the principal's office, or stuffed into a trash can by bigger kids. Riding the bus home with a black eye or a note from school, damp and stinking from all the spit and spilled milk in the trashcan, I wanted to escape into the minimalist world of cartoons, a place where there was only enough scenery to tell you where you were, and whatever antagonists existed were easily spotted.

Where I failed, Bugs triumphed. He fought gangsters, using his superior intellect to force them into the gas stove, which he then lit. With neither crosses nor holy water he excommunicated vampires and witches. He abolished abominable snowmen and the Tasmanian Devil. He defeated dragons, raging bulls, and oversized gorillas.

Only once did he fail, that I recall. At the end of *Hare-Way to the Stars,* after saving Earth from Marvin the Martian's dreams of destruction, Bugs drops a container of instant Martians into the sewer. There's a splash of water. After a moment the concrete buckles, and little pink antennae sprout through the cracks. Bugs climbs out of a manhole and replaces the cover. He turns to look at the camera, screaming, "Run for the hills, folks, or you'll be up to your armpits in Martians." In the atmosphere of the time, this end seemed fitting.


When Bugs is shot into space in *Hare-Way to the Stars,* before he finds Marvin attempting to destroy the world and before he spills instant Martians into the sewers of what might be Manhattan, he finds the Russian satellite Sputnik. With the advent of nuclear weapons, the earth being destroyed was a very real fear, and the reference to Sputnik is perhaps a sign that Marvin is a metaphor for Russia. Marvin plans to destroy the earth because it obstructs his view of Venus, an idea almost as ludicrous as the name of his weapon, the Illudium PU-36 Explosive Space Modulator, or as ludicrous as any reason for destroying the earth would be.

Many of the cartoons depict this ridiculousness of war. Dance routines intermingle with fighting. A war is likely to break out into a baseball game. Bugs and Yosemite often draw larger and larger weapons until the idea of trying to out-weapon the other becomes ridiculous itself, an obvious reference to the Cold War and the idea of mutual assured destruction. When Bugs and Elmer recreate the same scene of trying to out-gun one another, the weapons eventually become flowers and candy, which leads to marriage, prompting the shift from *The Barber of Seville* to *The Marriage of Figaro.* In *Bunker Hill Bunny,* Bugs and Yosemite switch sides and raise their respective flags (labeled "We" and "They") in the other's fort, running back and forth until we no longer know which side they are defending or what they are fighting about.

Some evenings the scenes from inside my house sounded like the Tasmanian Devil had gotten loose, or that the war had finally come, everything we knew destroyed by Marvin the Russian. Other nights, not often, there was music, reminding my brother and me of the Barber of Seville episode. We whispered on these nights that the next scene should be the marriage of Figaro, and our father would carry our mother across some threshold, forgetting he had fallen in love with someone else. We could not imagine what she looked like because we could not imagine anyone prettier than our mother, with her long brown hair, and when we thought of this, our father, tired from working all day, seemed smaller as he sat watching the news, trying to ignore our mother's questions about where he had been and why he was home so late. Other scenes we wished for were the Wagner *Ring* trilogy, where Bugs-as-Brunnhilde rides the white horse and Elmer Fudd as Siegfried realizes too late that he loves her, only we didn't want it to be too late. No water dripping from the last rose petal. No final pool of light. Even at that age, we realized there was such a thing as an end.

In their constant wars, Bugs's antagonists were almost as versatile in their incarnations as he was. Yosemite Sam was a confederate soldier, knight, gold prospector, train robber, convict, pirate, and—his most reprised role—generic outlaw. Defeated time and again, he rarely gave up, though in the milieu of the cartoon world, when Sam did admit defeat or learn from his mistakes, it was often too late.

Elmer Fudd was hunter, barbershop patron, patient in a sanatorium, wealthy industrialist, and Royal Canadian Mounted Policeman. He had a gun but lacked the wit and daring of Bugs. Daffy was never anything but Daffy, and although his role was reprised often, he always seemed to find new lows to stoop to, attempting to sabotage Bugs or steal what did not belong to him. He never accepted defeat with grace, never learned from one episode to the next.

Bugs's enemies were his polar opposites. Bugs (in post-1940s versions) was calm, at ease with the world. Charles Jones once said his inspiration for Bugs was Cary Grant. Mel Blanc compared Bugs to the leading movie stars of the '40s: Clark Gable, Humphrey Bogart, Jimmy Cagney. He never lost his temper, never raged at the world like Yosemite Sam or Daffy Duck, who were always on the verge of breakdown, always in crisis. Jones said that Bugs was an aspiration, what we'd all like to be. Daffy, however, is who we really are, whether we want to admit it or not. After the drawing contest, a kid named Carl, who had also drawn something terrible, his caption misspelled, made fun of my picture. I knew even then that Carl was only projecting his disappointment at his own drawing onto me, but I decided that I would never draw again. I hated Carl, and art. Like Daffy or Yosemite or Wile E. Coyote, I wanted something more than what I had, even if I could not understand what it was.

Even now, the way the Bugs Bunny cartoons were created seems a magical process. First, a writer plotted out a script. Illustrators then drew the story's basic idea. The rough sketches were storyboarded, and the writers, illustrators, sound men, and directors collaborated, adlibbing lines and adding scenes.

When everyone agreed on the script, they recorded the dialogue, and once the dialogue was recorded, the director timed the action frames. The layout men physically staged the scenes. (In his book *That's Not All, Folks!* Blanc says it was not uncommon to walk into an office and see a man with an ax raised above his head and another man bent over ready to receive the blow.) When the layout was finished, the artists began penciling the approximately sixteen thousand drawings it took to make a single cartoon.

But I neither knew then, nor cared, how much work went into it. In the mornings it was enough for the images to roll past in coherent, magical order. To break down the cartoon into single drawings would have been to unravel the same world I am trying to understand now. Then, there was inherent danger in trying to figure out what had led us to where we were, in trying to make sense of the past. If I began, for instance, with my father working out of town, the next scene would be my mother sitting up late waiting for his headlights to sweep the wall as his truck pulled into the drive. The next scene might continue with low-throated conversations in the kitchen, conversations my brother and I could hear in our bedroom because they always began low and rose higher, causing us to cover our heads. Eventually we might get to a scene in which I watched the news with my father, his feet crossed in the reclining chair, and heard that President Carter had boycotted the 1980 Summer Olympics in Moscow. In the scene, I wouldn't understand the implications, but when the US severed relationships with Iran, where the fate of the American Embassy hostages was still unknown, my father said it seemed we were headed for war. After that would be the scene in which my father left for the last time, and then a shot of me walking slowly back inside to turn on the TV, hoping to find Bugs in Transylvania or Tasmania, somewhere so far away I couldn't imagine it on a map.

The cartoons, of course, never show what it's like for a marriage to disintegrate, unless it's the gorilla wife who hits her gorilla husband over the head with a rolling pin when he won't show love to the rabbit baby brought to her by a drunken stork.

And there were no children in the cartoons but for the two boys who watch the Road Runner and say "beep-beep zip-tang" in imitation of the noise the Road Runner makes.

Bugs reminded us we lived in a big, beautiful world, a world rich with all the wild imaginings of humanity—castles and kings, dragons and devils, Martians and angry men—a place where villains existed but heroes always won. But caught inside on another Saturday morning where cartoons were our only escape from all the anger and atrophy, we worried we would never see what waited in the world. We were too caught up in our own world, a family locked too far inside its own small history to see any outside it.

Perhaps the greatest example of the creation process of cartoons is the 1953 episode "Duck Amuck." Daffy Duck appears as a musketeer, but within a few frames the castle behind him is gone. He speaks to the animator, asking for scenery. The animator draws a farmhouse. Daffy, attempting to placate the animator, disappears off screen and reappears in overalls. He sings a few bars of "Old MacDonald Had a Farm," and the scenery changes to the frozen north. When he once again disappears and reappears, this time in snow gear, the scenery becomes the tropics. Daffy grows increasingly upset. He is completely erased. He is redrawn as a cowboy holding a guitar, only with no voice. His guitar rattles like a machine gun, and when he regains his voice, a rooster's crow comes out. When he finally gets his normal voice back, he is, predictably, raging. He asks for color in the penciled-in background, and the animator colors him in polka-dots. His body is erased and redrawn as a strange creature, with a flower-head and a flag for a tail. He is drawn as a sailor, then suspended over the ocean. The screen itself collapses on him, and he is given only a small stick with which to prop up the oozing blankness.

When Daffy finally loses control and demands that the animator reveal himself, we see that it is Bugs Bunny. It was often Daffy's contention in the cartoons that Bugs had somehow sabotaged him. He is never quite able to forgive Bugs his success. "Duck Amuck" was one of the first cartoons to break the fourth wall, to speak directly to the audience. It seemed to be asking who the characters were and if they were still characters when they had no body, or no voice, if they existed only at the end of an art pencil or paintbrush. It asked what a cartoon was and if it had any relationship to the world in which we live.

The cartoons asked us to suspend our disbelief. To watch Bugs Bunny was to believe all things were possible. Gravity could be denied simply by not looking down. A firearm could be thwarted by placing a finger in its barrel or moving the stock to the barrel end. Witches and kings and dragons and knights could all be defeated by the perfect application of intelligence and audacity. War could be ended by a marriage. The world could be saved by silliness.

Bugs never saved my parents' marriage or erased my fears of the end of the world, but he sheltered me from the worst parts of the divorce by offering an alternate reality—in eight-minute stretches anyway—from the too-real versions of our lives. Even Elmer Fudd knew it was all right to fail, for he did so again and again. Daffy could reattach his face every time it was shot off. Yosemite could blow himself up over and over, so maybe we might make it through the thrown dishes, and if we didn't, some song or dance or other art form—a badly drawn cartoon, for example—would offer enough hope to keep us going.

When everything seemed to be breaking down, I wanted to live in a world of cartoons. I wanted to escape through art, either the drawings of a world my brother and I could only imagine or the stories we told one another, the old lie that everything would be all right. I did not know then that I would come back to my childhood again and again, still trying to make sense of the absurdity we allow into our lives. As a kid I would have designed a world similar to the one in which Bugs Bunny lived; as an adult I know that is the dream of a child. There's no protection from failed marriages or Martians or from the missiles that might fill the night skies. There's no escape from men who want nothing more than to destroy the world, or, at the very least, kill everything in it. The only hope we ever have is to laugh, to create art that undermines our own destructive tendencies.

One scene that never made any sense to me as a child was Bugs popping out of a hole and consulting his map. He finds that he is not where he expected to be, exclaiming, "I knew I should have taken that left turn at Albuquerque!" At the time I wondered how someone as smart as Bugs could become so lost. Now, it seems fitting that Bugs often wound up in some place he did not expect. The place he finds himself in is always one of adversity, where he must devise some way to triumph despite unusual odds. Because in the end, we are always finding ourselves in some place we didn't expect to be, and we have to deal with where we have arrived. In the way only adults can, we are always lamenting the wrong turn we took, because without it, we think, our lives would have stayed inside the neat lines we'd designed.

A girl named Cheryl Miller won the art contest. I forget now what she drew but realized, upon seeing it, that she had talent and I did not. I would feel the same way years later, after taking a test for a gifted and talented program at our high school and being told I was neither gifted nor talented.

My parents kept fighting, and there was nothing I could do to stop it. Their shadows seemed cartoonish on the walls, but all I could do was watch. A few months after the art contest, I came home to find my father packing. He had pulled his truck up close to the front door of the house and was carrying out his belongings. When he told me he was leaving, I went inside and dug through my room until I found the picture of Bugs Bunny I had drawn. My lines were fat in places and too thin in others, and Bugs looked out of proportion. His grin was lopsided, his ears were too long, and his legs looked fuzzy. When I handed it to my father, I knew it was cheap and pathetic. I knew I had no talent, that I would never draw the world in which I wanted to live. But I gave it to him anyway, and he took it like it was something to be valued.

# The Full Moon

I'm still not sure of the chain of events that led to it, but my friends and I, around about eighth grade, began to show our asses. I mean this literally—riding to school with our older brothers or sitting at the back of the bus going to an away basketball game, we'd drop our pants and present our posteriors to someone behind us, our butts against the cold window for all the world to see.

This was at a time we considered "I'm With Stupid" T-shirts and making farting noises with a hand beneath our armpit witty repartee, so I'm not surprised we decided exposing ourselves was hilarious. We were navigating the minefield of junior high, before Facebook and cellphones and Miley Cyrus, and we decided to do that navigating with our pants down. I suppose the changing of our bodies and the deepening of our voices, the uncomfortableness of it all, drove us to extremes. If puberty made us miserable, then here was a way to counter the misery of it all. If our bodies had betrayed us, we would expose them for what they were.

Part of the reason we did this might have been that we saw so much of one another on a daily basis. In fourth-period PE and seventh-period Athletics, we were surrounded by nakedness, before and after class. Crammed into small locker rooms and given only a few minutes to change, there was no way to hide what was happening to all of us, the pimples and pubic hair, the unpleasant smells, the wild swing of emotions. Raise your head from lacing your shoes and there's an ass in your face. Look up from slipping on your socks and there's something else, vaguely sock-like, dangling in front of you.

I suppose, too, we might have been trying to make some mark. To rise above the anonymity of junior high, separate our faces—or at least our other end—from the crowd milling aimlessly on the front steps before the first bell, everyone dressed in the latest fad, notebooks scrawled with the names of friends as if to remind us we had some.

We started small, a quick flash in the locker room or on the basketball court after school, any time we wore pants with elastic waistbands. But soon the asses were everywhere. You'd be riding to school or home afterward, staring out the windows at the winter fields, breath fogging the glass, thinking about the uncertain future, and then bam, there's a butt flying by. Or you'd walk into the locker room after class and see a dozen pale moons pointed your way, as if you were the guest of honor and here was your salutation.

One Saturday night in our small town, we cruised the strip slowly, someone's older brother driving, Tommy and Shawn and I waiting for someone to tailgate us, to flash on the high beams, and when they did we beamed them back in unison. We spent the rest of the night pulling our pants down, and the following Monday, Tommy and Shawn escalated the adventure when they began mooning teachers in the classroom. When Mrs. Woolley turned to the board to diagram the gestation period of a giraffe, Tommy jumped from his seat, his pants already loosened, then spun and flashed the teacher's back before plopping down again. Shawn waited until Mrs. Scheel was fast-forwarding past the sex scene in Romeo and Juliet, then flashed a moon of his own.

From then on, nowhere was safe. In the hallways, in the parking lots, in the toy aisle at Walmart. On church buses and school buses and team buses, the smell of sodas and sweat accompanying us. We flashed the police station and the high school and the Methodist church. We mooned the baseball field in summer and ran through the empty halls of school when we'd stayed late after practice, exposing ourselves to the class-rooms we hated, to the principal's office, to all the trappings of the stifling institution that was junior high. We knew even then we were being herded, groomed for the corporate world or the factories or the military, depending on which track our test scores indicated. At a time when we couldn't even keep our asses covered, we were expected to make decisions that would affect our future selves, whom we thought about only when left alone for a moment after coming home to our cold houses, our empty rooms that looked out on frost-bitten fields, the grass turned brown now with winter.

The only way to counter the changes inside us was to show our disdain for the world around us, we thought, so we mooned the civics teacher when she forced us to be aware of that chang-ing world. The Cold War was still cold as ever, ten thousand intercontinental ballistic missiles standing ready to fill the night skies, enough nukes to destroy the world a dozen times over. There was crack in the inner cities and cocaine in the high-rises. Reagan invaded tiny Grenada to make us forget our terrible loss in Vietnam, AIDS was devastating Africa, and our parents told us the economy was going to hell in a handcart. We were already afraid of the changing world within us, and we now began to fear the world outside us as well, so we showed our asses to any agent of order: our Sunday school teacher and our principal and our parents, the game and fish commission officer, the army recruiter, the meter maid.

We snuck out of our houses late at night and hid in ditches and rose up to flash the passing cars. We withdrew from Wednesday night church and mooned the stained-glass windows where Jesus wallowed on the cross.

And one fall evening, after our parents had dropped us off at a school dance and we'd become bored with the same girls we'd known all our lives and the same tired songs played at all the dances, Tommy and Shawn and I went walking through the streets of town. This was something we did often, when we spent the night with one another, after our parents had fallen asleep and we had already talked about what we would do if we ever escaped our town. We went past the elementary school we'd been in only a few years before, past the swing sets and the jungle gym and the muddy fields where we played kickball. On the other side of the school, we went down Sixth Street as a slight wind stirred the tops of the trees. The houses were quiet, picture windows spilling light down into the yards as people sat in front of their TVs, faces changing from light to dark. Already we were headed for what we would become, the fights with parents, the sudden rage at anything and everything, the disinterest in school.

Tommy and I were walking in the middle of the street when we realized Shawn was crossing the yard of the nearest house, staying to the shadows. When he went through the streetlight, we saw him clearly for a moment, laughing as he climbed up on the front porch. Through the big picture window, we could see an old man and woman watching TV. Shawn unbuttoned his pants. He turned away from the window, then took a few steps backward, placing his ass against it. He looked up at Tommy and me and smiled, then reached back to rap on the glass.

The word *moon* has been a common metaphor for buttocks since the eighteenth century. The verb *to moon* has meant to expose to moonlight since the seventeenth century. Mooning dates back to ancient times as a way to shame an enemy or to offer insult. There are also variations, such as the sun and the salad bowl, but we stuck to the basics. We would not be crass. Mooning was a form of art; sunning could get you a rap sheet.

The first incident of mooning ever recorded was in 80 CE, when a Roman soldier mooned Jewish pilgrims on their way to Jerusalem, causing a riot and an aggressive response from the Roman Army.

At the Siege of Constantinople in 1204, the Greeks exposed their bare buttocks to the Crusaders after they expelled them from the walls.

During the Battle of Crecy in 1346, several hundred Norman soldiers mooned English archers; the archers retaliated with bowshots.

Anasyrma, a gesture of lifting the kilt or skirt, was used in Ancient Greece in connection with religious rituals, eroticism, and lewd jokes. The term is also used in describing corresponding works of art.

In 2006 a Maryland court determined that mooning is a form of artistic expression protected by the First Amendment as a form of speech, although we didn't know then that we were expressing ourselves. If we had rules, none of them were written down, but we didn't flash anyone with a visible disability or scar, the thought being that those people had been exposed to enough harshness already in life. We didn't flash children or hospitals. Spaces inside a church were off limits; church parking lots were not. Girls you wished to date were exempt; girls you had already dated were free game.

Now you can see an ass every five minutes on TV, but in the conservative '80s, that was not the case. We'd not yet been exposed to internet porn or even the *Victoria's Secret* catalogue with its waifish "angels" pouting in pink lace thongs.

In other words, we didn't know our behavior had a long history. But those Normans who showed their asses to the French were riddled with arrows, the riot that resulted from the mooning in 80 CE killed thousands of Jewish pilgrims, and the walls of Constantinople eventually fell to the invaders and the city was burned.

Which is to say that we might have learned a lesson, had we only known.


There were more people at the dance when we got back, out of breath, laughing so hard we could hardly stand. The lights were spinning and Wham or Madonna or Hall and Oates were playing while our classmates stood against the walls with their arms crossed, not looking at anyone else, somehow dreading both being there and leaving in that way only our early teenage years can produce. We crossed the corner of the dance floor and went up into the bleachers where the lights didn't reach, trying to hide, already sure something was coming for us.

After Shawn tapped on the window, the old man and woman looked around as if they'd never heard a tap on the glass before and didn't know where it was coming from. In the glare of the TV, they couldn't see out the window. They both squinted. The woman put on her reading glasses. Tommy and I stood in the yard, feeling something between shame and elation. Shawn was showing his ass, but he had also just given a great big moon to the world we couldn't control, exemplified by this old couple who sat washed by the glow of the TV on a Saturday night, who, instead of embracing the great world outside the window, had chosen to lock themselves behind it. Instead of looking out, they were looking in, as everyone did in our small town. Or so it seemed at the time. It was really just two old people who couldn't see without their glasses, but you can't explain that to a thirteen-year-old boy who has too many emotions rolling around inside him, too many fears for the future, too many pimples popping up on his once-clear skin, too much hair in formerly bare places.

By the time the old man stood and took a few steps toward the window, Shawn was pulling his pants up, but either the old man had come close enough to see or Shawn's butt left prints on the window. I didn't know then whether or not a person could be identified by butt prints, but when I saw the old man say something to his wife, who picked up the phone, I began to think that maybe instead of showing our complicated teenage psyches to everyone around us, we were just acting like children who didn't know any better. And when we saw the police walk into the dance with their flashlight beams bobbing up and down clearly not in time to the music, I knew we were just children.

The police reported the incident to the school, and the administration got wind of the happenings. Not long after the dance, someone squealed on Tommy and Shawn's classroom strikes. They were called to the principal's office, and the very area of their bodies that had so often been exposed was struck repeatedly with a wooden paddle and then suspended for a week.

All of them, that is. Not just their asses. The principal decreed that anyone caught exposing himself would be expelled from school.

I suppose he had never been inside a locker room. Or he had forgotten what it was like. The decorum of the '50s, when he'd gone to school, had decomposed, fallen into disrepair. The nuclear family had become a family scared of anything nuclear. Because of that uncertain future, there seemed, for a time, no reason in the world not to show our asses. Or perhaps this has always been the way we act when we are faced with the changing of our bodies, and at some point after that change comes the realization that the world is full of men showing their asses, and has been so since the Greeks, who created the foundations of democracy but also occasionally lifted their togas to expose their nether regions when things didn't go their way.

But before that realization are the carefree years, the years of mad-mooning, when the only thing to worry about is when to strike next, when to make your mark on the world before the world ends itself or you are forced into whatever life has been chosen for you. It didn't matter that your credibility was cheapened by your pants being down, only that you did something people would remember you by. Ahead of you are the trappings of adulthood, the car payments and weed eaters, the tinkering around in the garage on a Sunday afternoon before falling asleep in front of the TV. The weight gain and hair loss, the back fat and bad decisions, the jobs you don't want working for people you don't like. But until then there's a boy on a porch with his pants down around his ankles, tapping softly on a big picture window, while an old couple refuses to remember what it was like to be young.

# Candy Cigarettes

In the late '70s, everyone smoked. My grandfather, a veteran of World War II and the Korean War, smoked Marlboro Reds, what he called the hard stuff. He started smoking in the army, when GIs overseas received cigarettes in their C-rations. He said he and the other soldiers smoked when they took a break from fighting, that cigarettes became a small comfort, a fire they could control.

My older uncle smoked Pall Malls. He had once been an all-conference athlete, and later he ran marathons, after he entered a treatment facility for alcoholism and got his life back on track, but when I was a kid, he smoked unfiltered Pall Malls. I still remember the red package, the unsmoked ends dissolving in the puddles of rain beside the porch at my grandparents' house. Forty years later, he would die of lung cancer, but back then it seemed that smoking was the only way he could control the anxiety that crept up on him when he wasn't drinking. He was a high school history teacher, and perhaps his own history got to him, in the way we sometimes can't sit still with ourselves without needing help to even out.

My mother smoked Virginia Slims. Virginia seemed a long way from rural Arkansas, so maybe she wanted to be elsewhere. She and my father divorced before she was thirty, and she was left to look after my brother and me, so perhaps she needed a small comfort of her own. Her voice was sore from screaming in the days leading up to the divorce, and in the evenings, with my father gone, she stood smoking at the kitchen window, wondering, I guess, if she'd ever get her voice back.

My father quit smoking before I was born, but I could still smell smoke on his skin. He worked for the National Forest Service before the divorce, and some days burned land to clear it of undergrowth. Sometimes, during the summer, these fires got out of hand, and my father was forced to contain them. At night, after the news reported all the other awfulness in the world—the latest kidnappings and conflicts—he would lean forward when the wildfires out West showed on the screen, knowing he might be called to fight them.

The world was always smoking, it seemed. There was the threat of war with the Soviets, and there were butt cans outside the Walmart. More cans stood at the end of each aisle, a forest of bent cigarettes still smoldering in the sand. Crushed-out butts littered the floor of the grocery store, where my mother bought cartons of cigarettes at a time, and clouds of smoke eddied above us as we stood to check out. The teachers at my elementary school huddled outside in the rain while we were supposed to be napping, the smoke from their cigarettes climbing back in the windows and wrapping itself around us like the sound of the rain on the rooftops of our houses.

Behind the high school, the seniors stood by the smoking tree, hands cupped around lighters, heads lowered so their bodies formed the question marks their lives were becoming. When his girlfriend came to visit him at his house, my younger uncle locked himself in the bathroom to smoke, brushing his teeth afterward and claiming she only imagined the smoke seething from him. My mother smoked on the way home from work and when she stepped out of the car, a wave came with her, wrapping itself around my brother and me. It might seem strange to say so, but even now smoke smells to me like the comfort so many people around me were seeking then.

At the institute for individuals with intellectual disabilities where my mother worked, everyone smoked—from the secretaries and instructors to the residents themselves, sitting in the windows of the dorms where they lived, looking out at the buildings surrounding them and wishing they were anywhere but here. The staff smoked on break, standing outside in little groups, the ancient edifices rising above them like monuments to an earlier time. The institute had once been home to tuberculosis patients with disease in their lungs, and as an adult I realized that my mother had smoked because she could not get enough air in hers.

None of us could get enough air. Everything, it seemed, was awful, from the threat of nuclear war that we heard about every night to the mundane jobs our parents held, struggling to make ends meet. My mother sat at the kitchen table once a month with her bills spread out, running a hand through her hair and dragging deeply. She occasionally spoke of one of the institute's residents who had touched her heart in some way, but even those thoughts were tinged with tiredness. I could see it in her shoulders, in the way she smoked, staring at nothing for a few minutes before starting supper.

It's no wonder then that we started smoking. By the time my friends and I were teens in the '80s, we smoked for real, stealing from our parents' packs and circling our small town endlessly, looking for something to do. But even as kids in the late '70s, we asked for candy cigarettes. We bought bubblegum cigars. We didn't know that the makers wanted us to imitate our parents; we just wanted to hold our candy cigarettes in the same way they did. We sat out on the porch with the grownups and waved our smokes as they talked about the weather or war or the sorry state of the world. About their jobs and the failing economy and the high price of gasoline. We dragged on our cigarettes and blew out powdered sugar made to look like smoke, and we went to bed with sugar stuck to us in the same way my mother still has smoke from 1979 stuck to her skin.

Of course we tried to imitate those we loved the most. We wanted to understand what it was like to be an adult, as if we could get comfortable with the worries we would carry around the rest of our lives. We saw our parents struggling, and we saw the small comforts they found in what they sometimes called cancer sticks, as if death could also be a comfort, or at least something to laugh at because they were too tired to cry.

So we bought our packs of fake cigarettes, and the candy dust covered us. My brother and I tapped our candy cigarettes into our palms and squinted at the nightly news. My family sat all around, there in the den of my grandparents' house, and smoke eddied in the still air as we exhaled. It leaked from us like we would soon launch.

Years later, it occurred to me that everyone was trying to find some form of comfort, whether in candy or cartons of smokes. Airplanes were being hijacked and embassies overrun, and at any time, missiles might fall from the sky. Today, the world smolders again, as close to burning as it ever came in the '80s—wildfires in California and tear gas in cities. Protests on the streets of Kenosha and Portland and Pittsburgh, Asheville and Atlanta and Austin, because Black people can't breathe. COVID-19 has me thinking about what we draw into our lungs, and some mornings it all seems so much that I step outside to smoke, remembering how my family sat in the front room inhaling something that would soothe them. I wonder if they came from stronger stuff, because I can barely make it through a week with all the awfulness. They worked long hours at jobs they hated with the threat of the end hanging over them. They drove to work and back home and took us to practice and school plays and birthday parties and still managed to cook supper. They were tired all the time, broke and worried and scared, so they inhaled deep breaths of something other than air. Didn't matter that it was smoke, that it wouldn't sustain them. They were already burning up.

# Professional Wrestling Is Real

In 1985, less than six months after Ronald Reagan said, during a microphone check later leaked to the press, that the United States would begin bombing the Soviet Union in five minutes, the team of Barry Windham and Mike Rotunda, the US Express, fought a tag-team title match against Nikolai Volkoff and the Iron Sheik at WrestleMania 1. Mikhail Gorbachev had just been named supreme leader of the Soviet Union, and Volkoff, in Madison Square Garden, with the Cold War still as cold as we all suspected the Soviet Union to be, asked the crowd to stand for the singing of the Soviet national anthem. When he finished, the Iron Sheik grabbed the microphone to say Iran was number one and Russia was number one and then pantomimed spitting on the USA. A moment later, the music kicked on, and of course it was the opening chords of Springsteen's "Born in the U.S.A." as Windham and Rotunda came out, wearing silk jackets emblazoned with *USA*.

Windham, six foot five, somewhere around 260 pounds, had long blond hair, the type of hair an announcer might refer to as "locks" when calling Windham "Golden Boy." He hailed from Sweetwater, Texas, a place as American as apple pie and AR-15 rifles. Rotunda looked more working class, a man who drinks beer on the weekends while tuning his muscle car, listening to

Springsteen, and together they were the perfect team to represent America in the mid-'80s.

Against them were Volkoff, who was not Russian but Croatian, though no one cared to make such distinctions in 1980s America because one Soviet Bloc country was the same as another, and the Iron Sheik, who was neither iron nor a sheik. He had a name none of us cared to pronounce, but we didn't need to since he was from Iran and, coming off the Iran hostage crisis, our hatred toward his country ran high. It was enough to boo him, and we didn't need to know his name to do that.

I might also mention that WrestleMania was the most-viewed sporting event ever in the history of the world, a statement which is certainly not true, but seemed so to me at the time, though I couldn't watch it live because we had no way to order pay-per-view television, only a sad antennae that picked up two channels, one of which went to static any time a storm came over the blue hills. When the video was (finally) released, my best friend, Thomas—who had been calling the video store daily until the woman who worked there, exasperated, wrote down his number and said she'd call when it came in—rented it, and we watched it that night in his playroom.

In 1985, Madison Square Garden meant America. The crowd booing Nikolai Volkoff, his hand held up in a salute while he sang, reminded me how much hate we were supposed to have for the Soviet Union. I didn't fully understand the history of our hate, how the Cold War was, in a way, a continuation of World War II, which was a continuation of World War I. I only knew then that I even hated their weird-looking alphabet.

I also knew we hated Iran and the Iron Sheik's curly-toed shoes. We hated the hammer and sickle on the red flag Volkoff brought to the ring. We had been raised by parents whose parents had installed bomb shelters when they were children, or who at least made a tour of their storm cellar every spring to see if it would save them when the missiles began to fall. Like us, our parents held their hands over their hearts every morning and recited the Pledge of Allegiance. They sat through nuclear drills in elementary school, and they watched, breathless, as JFK called out Khrushchev in 1962 during the Cuban Missile Crisis. They had seen high school friends drafted and die in Vietnam, and though they might not have known about the colonial French aggressions that caused Ho Chi Minh to turn to China for help, they knew, behind all the rhetoric, stood Russia.

Thomas and I did not know that on this day the flames of our hatred would be fanned. The US Express came to the ring accompanied by the Boss singing about being born in the USA, a song we didn't understand was about all the ways America was shitty in the '70s and '80s and how many middle-class kids had no hope, because in the refrain the Boss keeps repeating he was born in the USA like it's something to be proud of. And we were proud as Windham and Rotunda battled the forces of evil, as Reagan had recently named the Soviet Union, and surely Iran was evil as well. We were proud as Windham, late in the match, golden-haired and big as a billboard in West Texas, grabbed Volkoff in a headlock and performed his patented bulldog maneuver, slamming Volkoff's big, fat, stupid Russian face into the mat.

But Volkoff and the Sheik were evil and, when the referee's back was turned, the Sheik hit Windham in the back of the head with manager Classy Freddie Blassie's cane, and Volkoff pinned him. The referee counted him out, 1-2-3, which in 1985 sounded like the countdown to a missile crisis. We would lose this war, we knew now, because the Soviets would fire first, or strike us

PROFESSIONAL WRESTLING IS REAL · 67

when no one was looking. If professional wrestling had taught us anything, it was that evil always cheated.

This was not the first time we had seen Volkoff or the Iron Sheik. Two years earlier the Sheik had been heavyweight champion. He had been wrestling for over ten years at this time, carrying his America-hatred spiel with him because the politics and propaganda of the time demanded it. American audiences didn't want to see an Iranian embrace our ideals—we wanted him to play the villain.

We saw Volkoff the same way. Volkoff had also been around since the '70s, starting with the name Bepo Mongol and wrestling as part of the Mongols tag team. In the mid-'70s he put on a mask and became the Executioner. He sometimes crushed an apple in his hand to show what he would do to his opponents. In the language of professional wrestling, he was a heel, an opponent the crowd is supposed to hate, a foil for the fan favorite.

In 1983 the Sheik won the World Wrestling Federation title from champion Bob Backlund. When he lost it a few months later, in 1984, Volkoff and the Sheik teamed up. Both were already hated, the Sheik because of his anti-American speeches and Volkoff for his Soviet background. Volkoff began singing the Soviet national anthem, and the Sheik spit at the mention of America. They both carried flags into the ring. They both saluted when Volkoff sang.

Without all this, they might have been loved. Both were men who came to America following a dream. Volkoff's grandfather was a champion Greco-Roman wrestler, and Volkoff wanted to carry on that tradition. The Iron Sheik was at one time a bodyguard to the Shah of Iran; after emigrating to the US, he

coached America's Olympic wrestling team, earning an ama-
teur championship for himself. Both were manly men, with big
muscles, full of machismo and masochism. Both carved careers
for themselves despite language and cultural barriers, and both
became celebrities in their sport.

The problem is that both came from countries America
didn't care for. We didn't know then that the US was helping
Iraq fight Iran, but the hostage crises and the hijackings of the
'70s and early '80s had taught us to fear anything Middle Eastern with the exception of Israel, a fear we would carry into the
early '90s and revive again in September 2001.

And both came from cultures we didn't understand. The
Iron Sheik's curly-toed shoes meant something, but we didn't
care to ask what. We didn't know the meanings behind the
heavy clubs he brought into the ring, or the headdress he wore,
or the colors of the Iranian flag. We didn't know the Cyril-
lic alphabet is based on Greek, brought to Christian converts
in Russia in the ninth century, meaning we shared at least the
beginnings of religion with the Soviet Union. Nor did we know
that the hammer and sickle stood for the proletariat and peasants, which might mean that the Soviet Union valued work as
much as we hardworking Americans did.

And both came up against Hulk Hogan, who embodied everything American, from the Aryan hair to the admonition to say
your prayers. After defeating Bob Backlund, the Sheik lost the
title to Hogan. In the way of wrestling storylines, the Iron Sheik
was the transition that allowed Hogan to rise to the top. Wrestling promoters didn't want Hogan to fight Backlund because
both were fan favorites, so enter the Iron Sheik, a man we could
all hate with impunity, a heel, a foreigner from a foreign country whose foreign name we wouldn't pronounce.

But of course, in our thirteen-year-old ways of looking at the world, we didn't know Hulk Hogan was a stage name as fake as Iron Sheik. Hogan was born Terry Eugene Bollea. He had been wrestling for a few years in the American Wrestling Association (AWA) and Japan, but Vince McMahon saw him as the face of the World Wrestling Federation, which he wanted to expand.

With Hogan, he did just that. Hogan was already a rising star. In 1982 he played Thunderlips, a professional wrestler in *Rocky III,* which foreshadowed Hogan's career. In the movie, he's a crazed wrestler who surprise attacks Rocky, like a heel would, but by the end, when the match is stopped, the two take a Polaroid together to show their mutual respect.

Hogan was still a heel when he first joined the WWF. But in 1984, on an episode of Championship Wrestling, Hogan saved then-champion Bob Backlund from a beatdown. Backlund explained Hogan's change of heart, and fans bought it. When Backlund lost the title to the Iron Sheik, Hogan won it weeks later. After the match, long-time commentator Gorilla Monsoon proclaimed Hulkamania was here.

It was. Hogan became the most popular wrestler on the planet. He was the first professional wrestler to appear on the cover of *Sports Illustrated.* He hosted *Saturday Night Live* and had his own cartoon. He was the most requested celebrity of the '80s for the Make-A-Wish Foundation. He told all of us to train, say our prayers, and eat our vitamins. I'm not sure what we were supposed to train for, since I already knew I would never stand six foot seven or weigh three hundred pounds.

Wrestling was on the rise as well, gaining popularity through weekly cable broadcasts and pay-per-view events, as well as through "The Rock 'N' Wrestling Connection" after Lou Albano and other wrestlers starred in Cyndi Lauper videos. WrestleMania had over a million viewers on closed-circuit TV. I have no idea how many people rented the video, only that Thomas and I watched it ten or more times, rewinding when Windham bull-dogged Volkoff, then crying foul when the Sheik hit Rotunda with the cane.

The USA versus USSR storyline was kept alive with Hogan. In October 1985 on *Saturday Night's Main Event,* which aired on network TV, Hogan met Volkoff. In a pre-match interview, Hogan, carrying the American flag and wearing a shirt that said "American Made," tells Mean Gene Okerlund that he can't stand to see our enemy's flag in the ring. After pinning Volkoff, Hulk takes the Soviet flag and spits on it. He shines his shoes with it. He listens to the chanting crowd. I turned thirteen that year and held all the insecurities of the age. I was still afraid the Soviets would rain missiles down on our heads, but here one of them had been defeated. The flag had been defaced. The fear, for a moment, was replaced by a sense of superiority, the same way I felt when the Wolverines rose from the rocks in *Red Dawn* to shoot the Soviets who had invaded their small Colorado town. In all our toxic masculinity, all we needed to feel less afraid was a man who could defeat other men. No wonder then that Hogan was our hero.

Hogan's feuds weren't the first in professional wrestling. Cow-boy Bill Watts, a wrestler-turned-promoter in the old Mid-South, created episodic, recurring feuds, such as when Jake the Snake and the Barbarian feuded with Dr. Death Steve Williams and Ted Dibiase, until the Barbarian turned on Jake the Snake after Jake, blinded, unknowingly dropped a DDT on his partner. The Midnight Express feuded with the Rock and Roll Express. Junkyard Dog feuded with Moondog Spot. Cowboy Bill Watts himself stepped into the ring after being insulted by Jim Cornette, fighting alongside a man named Stagger Lee, who was really Junkyard Dog in disguise.

The same year WrestleMania brought Hulk Hogan to closed-circuit TV all around the country, the National Wrestling Alliance (NWA) aired Starrcade 1985. Tully Blanchard and Magnum T.A. fought inside a steel cage in an "I Quit" match, wherein Tully screamed that he did indeed quit as Magnum tried to carve his eye out with a piece of a chair. Manny Fernandez and Abdullah the Butcher fought in a Death Match. Sam Houston and Krusher Kruschev fought, as did Dusty Rhodes and Ric Flair, whose feud would continue for years, culminating in a five-man event dubbed "Wargames," which took me back to 1983 and the Matthew Broderick movie about the end of the world.

The popularity of wrestlers was also predicated on more than just their feuds. The most famous wrestlers had a patented finishing move. The Iron Sheik had the Camel Clutch. Jake the Snake Roberts dropped the DDT. Macho Man Randy Savage hit people with the flying elbow, sometimes referred to as atomic, and Hulk Hogan had the Atomic Leg Drop, as if adding the word *atomic* to anything made it more dangerous, which we all knew it did, considering our country's finishing move would be to let the missiles fly when our great feud got unmanageable.

The US versus USSR storyline was one that would return throughout the '80s. The Cold War was everywhere: in our movies and military, in our games and aggrievances, in our politics and propaganda.

While Hulk Hogan was being a real American and vanquishing any threats to our flag in the WWF, in the NWA, the Russian Team of Don Kernodle (decidedly not Russian), Ivan Koloff, and

Nikita Koloff was trying to prove Soviet dominance. After losing the six-man tag team title, Kernodle, still not Russian, was fired and replaced by Krusher Kruschev. Fighting as an all-Russian team, they won the NWA World Tag Team Title twice. Nikita was called the Russian Nightmare, in contrast to Dusty Rhodes, nicknamed the American Dream. Ivan was the Russian Bear, and Krusher, I suppose, crushed things.

What we didn't know at the time was that not one of the Russian team was Russian. Krusher Kruschev, born Barry Allen Darsow, and Nikita Koloff, born Nelson Scott Simpson, went to high school together in Minnesota. Ivan was born in Canada with the name Oreal Donald Perras. The whole thing was invented, a plan contrived to convince us to hate.

It was all so confusing. We didn't know who to hate anymore. By this time it was 1988, and we were old enough to suspect, like so many other things we heard in the world, that wrestling wasn't real. Nothing was real anymore. The Soviet Union itself had changed: Mikhail Gorbachev was talking about opening up to the West, and Ronald Reagan was imploring him to tear down that wall. All our old hatreds were being questioned, but I wanted to hold onto mine, since holding on was easier than answering.

The AWA was just as confusing. Baron Von Raschke was goose-stepping around the ring like a German soldier of the Third Reich, but Raschke was really a mild-mannered American who had won a high school football state championship in Nebraska. He was a US Olympic team qualifier in wrestling. When he wasn't wrestling, he was a substitute teacher, and later in his life he starred in a play based on his time in the ring, in which he claimed the fans hated him so much he often had to fight his way out.

I'll say that we did. We hated Von Raschke, with his claw and German goose-step. And the Koloffs, with their one-piece wrestling tights with CCCP, whatever the fuck that meant, written on them. We hated Skandor Akbar and Kamala the Ugandan Giant and Kareem Mohammed, whose real name was Ray Canty. Akbar was from Texas. Kamala was from Mississippi. But their personas were of evil men, and we were quick to believe this because their skin was a different shade than ours or their accents shaped words in a different way. Because we already had swimming inside us some predilection to hate those different from ourselves if they offended us in any way.

In the mid-'80s, about the time the Soviet Union was showing the first signs of weakening, Nikolai Volkoff had a change of heart. After feuding with Hulk Hogan, he fought against Corporal Kirchner, an Eighty-Second Airborne Paratrooper, whom Volkoff defeated in a "peace match" on *Saturday Night's Main Event*. During their rematch, at WrestleMania 2 in 1986, Volkoff's manager, Classy Freddie Blassie, throws Volkoff the same cane the Iron Sheik used to hit Mike Rotunda the year before, but Kirchner intercepts. He hits Volkoff in the neck and pins him. While Volkoff rolls around on the mat, Kirchner raises the US flag. He leaves the ring to the tune of "The Army Goes Rolling Along."

A year later, at WrestleMania 3 in 1987, Volkoff and the Sheik are feuding with Hacksaw Jim Duggan, who interrupts Volkoff's rendition of the Soviet national anthem, all of which Thomas and I managed to watch via pay-per-view, though we were growing older and less susceptible to the pageantry of professional wrestling. I was already leaning toward the military, still harboring a great hate in my heart for the Soviet Union, no matter what Mikhail Gorbachev was doing.

Throughout 1987, Volkoff was partnered with Boris Zhukov, their team named the Bolsheviks, and they became something of a joke. They accrued loss after loss, including an infamous defeat in nineteen seconds at WrestleMania 6. They split up soon after. Perhaps Volkoff had learned a lesson. His storyline suggested he was tired of losing, tired of his Soviet inferiority.

Volkoff publicly fired Zhukov, then grabbed the microphone and began singing "The Star-Spangled Banner." His storyline became one of a defector, and he feuded with Sgt. Slaughter, who couldn't stand the thought of a Soviet being welcomed by the fans. Slaughter, once a real-life Marine drill instructor, said America had become soft and weak. When Saddam Hussein invaded Kuwait, Slaughter became an Iraqi sympathizer, saying he liked Iraq's brutal regime. Days after the Gulf War air campaign began, Slaughter won the championship from the Ultimate Warrior. He was immediately challenged by Hulk Hogan, who heard Slaughter had desecrated an American flag, and after being defeated by Hogan, Slaughter teamed with Volkoff's old partner the Iron Sheik, now that the Gulf War had reminded us how much we hated the Middle East.

After Hussein's invasion, we all hated Sgt. Slaughter as much as we had ever hated Volkoff and the Iron Sheik. I had enlisted in the military by then. During the Gulf War, I watched CNN in my dorm room and shook with rage and alcohol. The war was real, though the storyline seemed to have come from the same men who wrote for wrestlers: Hussein had once been a fan favorite, as America supported him in his '80s crusade against Iran. When he invaded Kuwait, he turned heel, and all the good guys of the world came after him, like when the wrestlers rushed the stage to stop a savage beatdown but ended up delivering one of their own.

Ten years later the United States would invade Afghanistan, just as the Soviet Union had in 1979. Two years after that, we would invade Iraq again, as if the old feuds always return, and it gets harder, year after year, to remember who the good guys are and who the bad guys are. I've spent most of my adult life wondering where we stand now, if we're the good guys or the bad guys, and the only comfort I can find in my childhood is that I was too young, too ignorant of the way the world works to question what we were then.

Art, if we can call professional wrestling an art, imitates life. Wrestling fans of the mid-'80s were embracing what we all felt. Our lives were precariously balanced between hatred and fear. We were looking up at the skies, terrified, and to fight that fear we wrapped ourselves in flags and hatred. It was easy to hate when we were told the people we hated hated us as well. The Soviet Empire was evil, our president said. We will begin bombing them in five minutes.

It was always five minutes from doomsday, and the clock was ticking. We needed Hulk Hogan to halt the advance of foreign fighters. We needed the storylines of good versus evil to distract us from the real war being waged, because we can only live with such fear in small doses. Hatred, however, we can channel. We can convert hatred into energy and aim that energy toward whatever we feel fit: foreign countries, foreign flags, anything we hold enmity toward in our small-minded fears.

The problem, of course, is that professional wrestling is fake. Nikita Koloff was from Minnesota, for God's sake, which means that whatever hatred we held for him was hatred for ourselves. We aimed our enmity at others, vilifying enemies to feel better about our own atrocities. I always feared Soviet missiles aimed toward us; I never wondered where ours were headed.

What wrestling came down to—what everything always comes down to—is the two biggest kids on the block vying for control of their corners of the world. Hogan versus Volkoff. The Russian Nightmare versus the American Dream. The good guys versus the bad guys. Us versus Them, as if all our endeavors come down to a simple binary. As if we didn't know better than to think that being the strongest means being the best.

Which may be why Hulk Hogan was so popular. Beaten down, bloodied, the Hulkster always rose. Shaking, sometimes willing himself to his feet, he fought back. Afterward, he waved the flag. He taught us all to say our prayers. To hold our hands over our hearts and never question our country, because the big bad Soviets were out there with their ICBMs. He taught a generation of young boys to grow up to be men who saluted symbols, who refused to acknowledge the storyline repeating itself in every wrestling match and every war on every continent.

It's a simple solution, to love symbols. Much easier than looking inside at what causes such enmity in the first place, why we're so disposed to hate. Why we build walls around ourselves, why we accept so easily that anyone outside our own small spheres is worthy of our suspicion.

I'll say now I sympathize more with the bad guys, not because of any country of origin, but because, night after night, they endured hatred and harassment. Skandor Akbar had to wear a bulletproof vest to the ring. Baron Von Raschke had to fight his way out. Volkoff and the Iron Sheik caused so much hate in our hearts we cursed their foreign names and their foreign cultures and their foreign countries. It doesn't matter they weren't the personas they wore in the ring, because most of the stories we believe are so contrived as to be ridiculous, written by men in back rooms as a way to make money and expand their empire, pushed on us by propaganda as silly as the stories in professional wrestling. Despite this, the fighters kept coming every night, maybe hoping, at some point, we would realize they were pawns just like us, all stuck following the same script, trying to find some way in this world before the final bell rang.

# Arc

This is a story about a mouse whose death taught us what it means to live. It's a story about a mouse as a teacher. About a mouse and a teacher. And a trial. This is a story about all the ways we don't understand what we've done until after we've done it. It's about a murder and a funeral. It's also a metaphor, because even a mouse can be a metaphor, if looked at in the right flash of light.

At 1:23 p.m. on November 7, 1989, we condemned the mouse to die. But, like all good stories, its beginnings have earlier roots. And like all good deaths, it begins with a lesson.

This one was on electricity. It was also on the end and what happens to our synapses when we're gone. It was a lesson that began with the idea that all our human interactions are electrical. All our brain waves and muscle movements, all our hopes and dreams, are simply little arcs of electricity shocking us into existence.

We'd been learning about muscles in Mr. Prewett's senior science class. It was fall, but we were already leaning toward graduation and getting out of this godforsaken town, as well as getting out of the '80s altogether. We liked the music videos but hated the missiles. We liked Swatch watches and acid-washed jeans but hated the atmosphere of fear we all walked around in, so we were aiming ourselves elsewhere, not knowing at the time we'd always be circling back to see what we were once like, trying to understand how we ended up the way we are.

Mr. Prewett wore glasses so thick we said he could see the future. Really he just observed the present, and what he saw through his thick lenses were teenagers tired of worrying about their futures but too tough to admit it, so they adopted a degree of indifference that kids have been carrying around since the first synapses of the first one arced into adolescence.

So one afternoon when we weren't paying attention, as Mr. Prewett tried to explain to us how electrical impulses that originate in the brain drive all bodily functions, as our eyes glazed over and we thought of college or summer or what we would do after school that day, as he could see us slipping away toward wherever we would go after we left here, he said, "Electricity can even stimulate muscles after death," and, when that didn't fully arouse us, "That's why men convulse when they're electrocuted."

I assume now he meant in movies. We did not think Mr. Prewett had seen an execution, though we would have, at that age, liked him more if he had, even though we already liked him very much. We had taken his ninth-grade class too. We had done the egg-drop experiment, climbing to the top of the football press box and dropping our contraptions fifty feet, most of our eggs exploding, reminding me now how difficult it is to convey a concept, like an egg or an idea, across such vast distances. Earlier in the year he had taught us vectors, which I don't remember much about, except how they can determine the position of one point in space relative to another, which is what writing in general and this essay in particular are about.

But we were past learning. We were in our senior year, and Mr. Prewett knew we were just marking time. He knew his days of teaching us something new were over, so some afternoons he let us play that paper football game or that game where we broke each other's pencils. Some days we told jokes about how stupid the Soviets were, and some days we had put-down fights, though no one ever beat Mr. Prewett. I came close once when I said, "You're so ugly you have to trick-or-treat by mail," but he responded that I was so ugly I could make a train take a dirt road, and though I'd like to rewrite the scene so I say, "You're so ugly when you throw a boomerang it doesn't come back," that didn't happen, and Mr. Prewett remained king of the put-downs.

So in this soft, liminal space before we eased into the rest of our lives, Mr. Prewett said he could prove it.

"Prove what?" said someone, maybe Mike Bryant or Jerry Bradley.

"That muscles move by electrical shock," he said, pausing just long enough that we were leaning forward, "even after death."

In the eager quiet that followed, the kind I've gone looking for in every class I've ever taught, Mr. Prewett laid out his plan: we would need a test subject, a mouse or a frog or a snake. We would kill it, then hook a small electrical generator to it and send pulses through its body to see its muscles move. We had to kill it in class, he said, because the body only responded to the impulses for a few minutes. After that it was over. Finished. Final. Finito.

I'd like to say there was a moment where we realized the monument of death stood before us, but the collective momentum had not yet struck. As these things go, it would not until years later, when the mundane is rendered monumental, and all our molehills become mountains.

In the silence, Daniel Simpson said he could catch a mouse in his barn and bring it to school the next day. Mr. Prewett told us he had the rest of the equipment, which made us wonder what chemicals and compounds lingered behind the always-locked door in the science room. But the bell rang, and we filed out. When we filed in the next day, Daniel had a mouse in a big glass jar with holes poked in the lid, and we stood around while it sniffed the air inside and put its little paws on the side of the glass as if looking for a way out.

It was at this point that the first objection was raised. Heather Hall, who now has a child older than we were back then, said she didn't want to see it die. Some wit offered she could always leave, but she raised her objection further—we could not kill this creature, she said. It would be inhumane. It would be immoral. We knew what would happen when the impulses hit its muscles because Mr. Prewett had told us, and none of us needed to actually see it happen.

I'd like to contend that Heather was wrong. That we—and by "we," I mean we humans walking around wondering what we are doing on this earth—need to see death. That even though we see it every day, we still don't understand the electricity that flows through us or what happens when it stops, which is, ultimately, what everything is about. Every little fear we felt, from the Soviets to the Satanists to the people who put razor blades in apples or kidnapped teen girls off the streets, started out as a little arc of electricity.

So a chorus of voices shouted Heather down, and that might have been the end of it, but Mr. Prewett, whose glasses were not quite thick enough to show him the future, said if there was one conscientious objector we had to take that into account. Maybe he was as bored as we were, ready to head into summer and the freedom it brings from little shits like us, or maybe he saw some lesson we didn't—maybe he knew death isn't the ultimate lesson, only what happens after.

So when someone suggested we have a trial to determine the mouse's fate, Mr. Prewett agreed. This was during the time *L.A. Law* was teaching us all what it meant to be a lawyer, so Mr. Prewett said Heather would be the defense. Matthew Foy was named prosecutor, and Cliff McAnally and Sherry Wann were the judges. We would have opening statements the following day, and the mouse would have a short reprieve until then.

And look, I don't remember all the arguments Heather and Matt made the next day. Matt teaches high school music now, and I doubt he's ever dealt with the death of a mouse in his classes. If I had to guess, I'd say he doesn't use those humane mousetraps at home or drive captured mice out into the woods to be released. Heather's big mistake, if I remember correctly, was assuming that we all shared her morals, when in reality we were, like far too many of us now, trying to find some entertainment, even at the expense of others. We were scared all the time—of losing our aging grandparents, of the rising fanaticism in the Middle East, of the rising fanaticism here at home—but here we didn't have to be afraid because we weren't the one about to die. I remember making a point to ask why we got the mouse in the first place, as if to remind everyone. I remember asking Mr. Prewett if he thought lessons about how our brains control our bodies were important, if learning about death was important to learning about life.

What I'm saying is, I wanted the mouse to die. I framed my questions in such a way as to help Matt in his prosecution. I used words to move the class toward the verdict I wanted, which is what I'm doing now. There's a verdict coming, and it isn't the one you think it is, because we can't ever see it coming until it gets here, which is what scared us so much back then about Intercontinental Ballistic Missiles.

But I wanted to see it happen, there in the classroom. I didn't yet know what it was like to lose something. I was sad for reasons I can't recall. Maybe because of the Cold War, the missiles beneath our feet that could be above our heads in minutes. Maybe because of all the stories we heard in church about death and eternal life, how one day we will die and we better be prepared for what happens after. I'm sure most of these reasons seem now so small they couldn't even fill the holes Daniel had poked in the jar lid, but maybe we need to see suffering to understand why we are so unsettled. Maybe we need to see the last throes of death to understand life. Maybe we constantly need to revisit the past in an attempt to see the future.

And I don't want to belabor the point, so let me just say that Heather lost. Cliff and Sherry went out into the hall and came back in with a death verdict. They didn't publish their opinion, but I'd bet all the mouse shit that had accumulated in the bottom of the jar that it would have said they just wanted to see the mouse die.

When the verdict came back, Heather asked to be excused from class. Mr. Prewett, who later said the whole situation turned out to be an important lesson on moral values, along with learning about the electricity that runs through us and makes us what we are, took some chemical—formaldehyde, maybe, or some other compound back there in that locked room with the beakers and burners and powders and potions—and soaked a cotton ball with it. Daniel opened the lid, Mr. Prewett dropped the cotton ball in, and a few moments later the mouse curled up and died.

In my high school yearbook, there's a huge picture of Dustin Blankenship, my best friend on that day thirty years ago, shocking the mouse after it died. And it did twitch a little, as

Mr. Prewett told Dustin where to hold the electrodes. Its legs twitched when he touched it, and we took turns shocking the mouse until it eventually quit moving, no matter how high we turned up the machine.

And afterward, as men will, we turned the machine on ourselves. Mr. Prewett said the same principle worked with us as well, so we held the electrodes to our arms and watched our muscles jump, though perhaps we were only trying to feel something besides fear. Daniel held the electrodes up to his temples and said he could see flashes behind his eyes, and when Dustin held them to my knee I kicked a desk so hard it lifted up. For the rest of the class, while the mouse lay dead, we kept shocking each other, watching all our involuntary movements, all the ways we didn't know what we were doing, only following impulses sent to us from the thing atop our necks we still don't understand.

The truth is, there's always some electricity swimming through us, until there isn't. In the yearbook, Mr. Prewett is standing next to Dustin, guiding him. Another picture shows the funeral we held for the mouse. We buried him in a little box outside the science room. Kelly McClendon played "Taps" on her trumpet. Mr. Prewett read from Genesis that "unto dust shalt thou return." The funeral procession wound down the hallways of the old high school, past the typing classroom where the typewriters were ticking away, as if everyone inside had a story they wanted to tell.

So here's the story I want to tell: thirteen years later, after I had moved away and was learning how to write stories about the past, Mr. Prewett was hit by a car and killed one evening jogging along the main street of my small hometown.

The night he died, my mother called to tell me. And here's the way synapses in the brain work: they're still there, years later. Still firing and connecting and vectoring from one place to another, still reminding us we were once moved. So I told her about the mouse and the trial and the funeral, and after I finished, in that tender space somewhere between denial and acceptance, she told me he had died instantly, though maybe she just didn't want me to wonder whether the doctors tried to shock him back to life.

# Missile Command

I will admit now I was not the likeliest of heroes, but at age eight I saved the world more times than I care to count. This was 1980, and there were missiles everywhere: on the nightly news, in silos under our feet, circling the earth in submarines. Scientists assured us half the population would die in the initial explosions of a nuclear war, and another third in the radiation that came afterward, leaving only a remnant of humanity for the nuclear winter to come, where crops would die and no one could get a good suntan.

Which was why, every afternoon after school, I flipped the switch on my Atari 2600—a name that sounded like a future computer—and set about saving the world. On the black screen were six blue cities. A cursor served as an aiming reticle, and as small straight lines streaked toward the blue cities huddling far below, I fired bombs at the missiles to explode them in midair. In each wave, a dozen or more missiles streaked downward. In each wave, the missiles fell faster, finally coming so quick it was impossible to protect every city, so I had to decide on one or two to save, hovering the cursor over them, ignoring all the other strikes. Bombs intermingled with the missiles, and each city made a little mushroom cloud when hit.

I played until my parents came home. Until dark fell outside and finally my father wanted the TV, so he could turn on the news and see what awfulness had occurred that day between the United States and the Soviet Union, names that still seem so similar as to be the same.

After the news, we immersed ourselves in the images on the screen: Magnum PI helicoptering around Hawaii or the doctors of *M\*A\*S\*H* cursing death. In 1981 *The Greatest American Hero* came on, a show about a man with no particular abilities other than an alien suit, which he is supposed to use to fight crime but often crashes into walls because he lost the instruction manual. It seemed all of us had lost the instruction manual, that we were often crashing about or cursing death, wishing we were in Hawaii or some other place where we might be protected from the men in power. After the ten o'clock news told us again about all the danger in the world, my parents sent me to bed, where I lay awake wondering if I'd ever be able to fly or if the missiles would find me before I achieved all the greatness of superheroes, or at least the greatness of Magnum PI's mustache.

Sometimes, when I couldn't sleep for fear of the missiles flying, I'd sneak into the living room late at night. In the darkness I'd turn on the Atari, moving my cursor to stop the missiles, firing again and again. Late at night, everyone else in my world asleep, the cities would fall one after the other, as the missiles came faster and faster, each small city erupting into ruins because the missiles just kept coming, until all the cities were destroyed and the final scene showed an explosion big enough to shake the screen. The world goes red, then yellow, then black—to announce the end has finally come.

Those missiles streaking downward became a common theme of the '80s. In 1983 the movie *Wargames* was released, in which

Matthew Broderick stars as a tech-savvy kid who inadvertently starts the countdown to World War III while playing a computer game. After hacking into the mainframe of the War Operations Plan Response computer, or WOPR, a computer that spends all its time, according to the technician in the movie, thinking about World War III, Broderick loads a game of *Global Thermonuclear War*. He is offered two choices: the US or the USSR, but the computer can't tell what is real and what is simulation.

A few years before *Wargames* was released, my school got its first computers, Commodore 64s with green screens and, from what I remember, no operating system to explain their use. By 1983 we had Tandy 1000s, and we all wanted to hack into the mainframe like Broderick (there was no mainframe, dear readers) and change our grades, but what we did instead was learn simple programming. We wrote:

```
10 PRINT "PAUL LOVES JENNIFER"
20 GOTO 10
```

And saw our names repeated endlessly on the screen, but soon grew bored with ourselves, no matter how many times our names appeared. The games we had at school only taught us math or vocabulary. We wanted *Global Thermonuclear War*, because already inside us was a delight in destruction, or maybe we only wanted to scare ourselves so others couldn't. At that age I was scared all the time, from the Baptist minister on the nightly news who said the world would end in fire to the nightly news and movies telling us how it might happen, and to fight that fear I wanted to either save or destroy the world.

Luckily for us, a boy I'll call Chuck knew as much about computers as Matthew Broderick and brought us video games like *Zork: The Great Underground Empire* and some maze game with a character more like a Monopoly piece than a person. Both games were slow and frustrating, but still better than third grade. Rainy afternoons when we couldn't go to recess, we shoved each other to get to the computers first, then loaded *Zork,* a text-based game that told us, on the opening screen, that our unnamed player was standing in an open field west of a white house. We played by typing commands: */walk /climb /go down stairs /kill troll.* Each typed command unrolled more of the described world, assuming we could find the right words to do the unrolling. By circling the house—*/east /south /west*—we came upon a window slightly opened, through which we must */enter.* Inside the house stood a door with strange gothic lettering and a staircase that led to pitch darkness where we were warned, if we typed the command to go that way, that we were likely to be eaten by a Grue. Beneath an oriental rug lay a trapdoor, and below the trapdoor the Great Underground Empire spread out, a world of treasures and trolls, and with only simple commands, a sword of great antiquity, and a lantern lying on the table, the player ventured forth into the darkness.

What drew me to the game was the unknown of the Great Underground Empire, a phrase that conjured images of vast lairs lurking beneath my feet. In those lairs lay treasure—a jeweled scarab, a silver chalice, a clockwork canary—though I was more interested in escape: from the oppressiveness of church, the monotony of school, the very real fear of the end. In the Great Underground Empire, I thought, we might be able to survive the missiles falling.

Anywhere was better than where we were. In 1983 the wargames were real. In West Germany, US forces were maneuvering tanks through mock battles in an exercise known as Autumn Forge. Forge was followed by Able Archer, which simulated the use of tactical nuclear weapons by NATO following a Warsaw Pact chemical attack; according to recently released reports, the Soviets believed the attack was real, and imminent.

Because of all this, *Missile Command* no longer interested me. The threat seemed too real. In the movie, Matthew Broderick teaches the computer that no one wins a wargame, but I wondered how men, with all their misgivings, might ever learn. At the end of the movie, as the missiles on the screen are streaking downward and no one knows if they are real, we all wondered what would happen when they hit. In a scene that still scares the hell out of me, the missiles strike, one after another after another, giant white circles appearing on the screen until it is all blanked out, all the countries of the world, and nothing is left but what the Baptist minister told us the afterlife would be like.

To escape this fear, I stayed in the Great Underground Kingdom of *Zork*. A troll lived there, and that Grue-thing that would eat me, but I preferred the danger of the darkness to what might fall on us out of the sky. If I couldn't play *Zork,* I programmed my name to appear forever on the screen, hoping it might last. Outside, the rain fell endlessly it seemed, puddles appearing on the playground, the sky so gray the nuclear winter might have come. The fluorescent lights flickered overhead, but I was underground, like the rest of us, muddling my way through darkness.

In *Destiny 2,* an online game I play now, guiding my character through what looks like an abandoned, burned-out mall reminds me of the mid-'80s. Saturday mornings we woke early and drove an hour to Central Mall in Fort Smith, where my mother shopped in Sears and JCPenney, my year-older brother went to Walden's bookstore, and I disappeared into the arcade. Along the wall, Donkey Kong was throwing barrels at precursor Mario, who'd later invade our homes on the Nintendo Entertainment System, but now he was trying to rescue Pauline, who'd been captured, King Kong style, by a great ape. Next to *Donkey Kong* were *Galaga* and *Gauntlet, Tempest* and *Tetris* and *Tron, Dragon's Lair* and *Defender.*

Everywhere were blinking lights. Beeps and buzzes from the machines, the clack of quarters, the drone of teenage voices that hung in the air. I still get a brainless squirt of adrenaline remembering trying to fit a crumpled dollar into the change machine, a longing in the pit of my stomach for the joysticks oily from kid's fingers coated in pizza grease from Geno's Pizza by the Slice. The thin carpet frayed in front of the best games, where often a crowd gathered around a good player to watch them work.

Because I never had much money, most often only four measly quarters, four small chances to immerse myself in another world, I walked through the arcade a dozen times, trying to decide what to play, whether I wanted to save the world from missiles or save myself from asteroids. I did not know then how video games would affect me forty years later, how safe a digital world can seem, even one full of burned-out malls and monsters so big they can't fit on the screen. Every bowling alley or pizza place I've ever been in, I've gravitated to the *Galaga* game standing alone in a corner, or *Ms. Pacman* with her pink bow, or—holiest of holies—*Missile Command* with its trackball and red button. I still run my priest through the world of *Warcraft* trying to heal its wounds, or at least the wounds I feel when I'm not occupying myself in some other world. I still send my warlock into danger in *Destiny* to avoid thinking about the very real danger lurking in every corner of a world that's become an

'80s arcade: bright and blinking but with little substance we can see, a world hiding behind the screens of social media, where we offer little more than an avatar, as if we have become more character than content.

Even *Frogger* seems prophetic to me now: a lone frog trying to make its way across a busy street, only to be flattened by a car going too fast. *Pacman* tries to consume as much as he can, a perfect metaphor for malls of the '80s or the 1 percent of Americans who have way more than they need. *Space Invaders* and *Galaga* reminded us to stay afraid of something coming out of the sky. *Berzerk* introduced robots gone crazy because of artificial intelligence, the kind we are now striving to put into all our weapons systems, and *Asteroids* taught us we were all in a small spaceship floating through the endless void of space, waiting to be smashed to pieces.

In contrast came *Rampage,* which grew to be one of my favorite games. In it, the player chooses between a Godzilla look-alike, a King Kong wannabe, or a werewolf named Ralph. The goal is destruction: to tear down as many cities as possible before the puny humans and their militaries kill you, turning the tables on the old story that we had to save the earth and its cities. Much more fun to destroy, *Rampage* taught us. If the world is going to be destroyed anyway, the game seemed to say, we might as well be the ones to do it. It never occurred to me, of course, that since all the monsters in *Rampage* had mutated because of what men had done to them, that we had, once again, brought about our own destruction.

When my dollar ended, I'd gather around the guy who was close to saving Princess Daphne in *Dragon's Lair,* an animated game that looked more like a cartoon and required quick reflexes to keep Dirk the Daring alive as he moved through rooms fraught with danger. Or I'd watch four guys playing *Gaunt-*

*let* at once, a game I loved but in which the only goal seemed to be to get out alive.

I never wanted to leave. Sometimes, holding onto to my last quarter, or feeling inside each machine's coin return to see if any forgotten quarters were hidden there, I'd close my eyes for a moment and let the sensations wash over me: the bells and whistles from the pinball games in the back, the confusion of popcorn and cotton candy and recycled air, the vast empty chaos of the place.

When time came to meet my mother, I'd walk slowly through the sad stores. The noise of the crowd never seemed as lifelike as the sounds in the games I played, the lights never as bright as those on the screen. I didn't know then that the death of the arcade had already begun. The Atari console I loved so much would be replaced by the Nintendo, and soon consoles and home computers would choke out the arcade in the same way online shopping and big box stores would begin choking out the malls across America, leading, in my imagination, to the mall in *Destiny 2*, abandoned, burned out, trees and vines growing in the corridors, inhabited by monsters, though the monsters in my imagination are the ghosts of young kids, all grown now, wandering around looking for the arcade.

Enter now Nintendo, which I first saw at Michael Wilkins's house one afternoon maybe ninth-grade year, which means 1987 or so, me at the tender and adolescent age of fifteen. Being the video game junkie that I was, I noticed Michael's NES as we stopped at his house before basketball practice and, even though we only had a few minutes before wind sprints started, I forced Michael to turn it on. The cartridge in the NES was *Mario Golf,* and there was Mario from *Donkey Kong* playing golf, a surprising turn of events in itself, but I remember gaping at the graphics. The only home console cartridges I had seen came from Atari, and its small sad missiles seemed, well, small and sad compared to Nintendo's, which were almost life-like, or at least more life-like than the triangles and rhomboids that made up most of Atari's games.

Michael let me play a couple of holes while he grabbed his socks or jock or unwashed shorts, and we headed back to practice, where I wandered around in a daze, missing shots and throwing the ball away until Coach Beckham sent me to run suicides. I was thinking of graphics. I hated golf, but I could already imagine the possibilities of playing characters that didn't look cut from digital cardboard, trees that were more than a green polygon.

At school we were still playing computer games. In the way of what were called auxiliary courses, Coach Bailey's computer class had no common core to follow, so Coach didn't much care what we did, since, as he said, whatever he taught us about computer programming would be outdated by the time we graduated anyway. We spent the first few weeks programming simple slideshows and tutorials for Coach's class, then were given what Coach called an open agenda, by which he meant we were free to work on whatever computer programming skills we saw fit, but which we took to mean free time.

So we played *Leisure-Suit Larry in the Land of the Lounge Lizards*, an R-rated game in which Larry tries to get laid as often as possible, but, in true late-'80s style, dies if he forgets to wear a condom when he commandeers a prostitute. We played some stock market game in which we tried insider trading our way to being a millionaire, buying short and hoping the market jumped, though if we lost it all we only had to restart. Like all the investments of our lower-middle-class families, our offerings were little more than hope: for the market to hit, for our short sells to go long, for our investments to return tenfold.

We played *Where in the World Is Carmen Sandiego?* And *The Oregon Trail,* where everyone died of dysentery, and *King's Quest,* which had us wandering around an open world looking for treasures that would save the kingdom. Its interactive world—point-and-click games we call them now—was one of the first of its kind, and the graphics, though horrendous by today's standards, allowed us to immerse ourselves further in the imaginary world of Daventry kingdom, where daggers were hidden in holes and golden eggs waited in high trees.

By junior year we were playing *MechWarrior,* which I thought at the time was the greatest video game ever made. The main character is Gideon Braver Vandenburg, whose family has been murdered, and something something about a chalice. No one really cared about the storyline, because the game play had Gideon piloting a BattleMech, a mechanized vehicle that looked like a forty-foot-tall suit of armor. Safe inside, the player controlled his mech, firing missiles and machine guns and lasers. The plot had Gideon trying to track down the Dark Wing Lance, who had supposedly murdered his mother and father and maybe sister and brother. Gideon creates a squad of BattleMechs to take his revenge, and he does this by becoming a mercenary, selling his Mech skills to the highest bidder of the five houses, entangling himself in their politics and something something something.

I forget. It was enough to pilot a Mech. To see the lumbering slow steps as they started forward, to fire lasers as the first enemy appeared over the horizon. It was enough to wrap myself in a massive suit of armor, to be protected from all but the greatest harm. The missiles and machine guns could destroy tanks and buildings and other mechs if the pilot was good enough, if he controlled his weapons and didn't overheat, if the missiles locked on target.

Outside the windows, missiles were still locking onto targets. That summer Ronald Reagan would beseech Gorbachev to tear down that wall, and it seemed the Cold War might finally end. But from Central America, word had come that our government had done some shady dealings. Crack had appeared in the inner cities and Oliver North was testifying before congress and the investigative journalists of the day said it all ran together, along with selling arms to Iran, our enemy, engaged in a war with Iraq, whom we supported with economic aid, military intelligence, and, rumor had it, weapons of mass destruction.

Safer to stay in here, we thought. The high school locker rooms were full of hairy men swinging fists at one another. Every argument broke out into a fight. The halls were full of adolescent teens trying to find their way in the world, which always ended in confusion, so each clique hid out where they could: the yearbook staff in the darkroom, the football players in the fieldhouse, the computer gamers in Coach Bailey's class, maneuvering giant Mechs through a world filled with agendas and assassinations, with shady dealings and double crosses, a world where men had to wear suits of armor to survive.

That Christmas I got a Nintendo, and Thomas and I played it all through winter. Many nights we fell asleep with the game still going, and even now I feel an overlapping of time when I hear the opening music to *Super Mario,* or the haunting melody playing in the background of *The Legend of Zelda.* Those tinny notes hit for me some sweet spot of nostalgia and melancholy: for a time long gone; for the simple act of immersion into another world without the cares and fears of this one; for the way we all, even those of us careful with our words, roll entire decades into a zeitgeist of music and politics and cultural icons when all we really mean is the way we felt.

What video games made me feel is hard to define. In the way of adolescence, awkwardness had appeared all over us. My parents had divorced, and Thomas's parents were heading toward it, so we hid out in the back room and avoided everyone but Thomas's younger brother, whom we beat up any time he ventured near. In video games, we attempted to escape, certainly, but in the escape was not only a desire for a new world. There was a desire for a better one, which was how I saw the land of Hyrule in *Legend of Zelda,* or Planet Thebes in *Metroid.* Both were dangerous, with all the monsters men can create, but in each one was a way to vanquish all the evil that existed. In each one was a way to save the world.

We played until late every weekend night, and when summer rolled around, we never went to sleep until gray light was leaking in the windows and our parents were waking up for work. Then we slept, while on the screen the music played or text unrolled with a sound like a typewriter, and sometimes I woke wondering what had called me awake, always saddened that I was still in this world and not another, where the rules were clear and whatever danger existed was easily overcome.

So we tried to lift Dracula's curse in *Castlevania.* We killed a resurrected Hitler in *Bionic Commando,* a game which had us swinging across great gaps using a bionic arm / grappling hook. In *Mega Man,* we took down Dr. Wily with his mega-robot plot to take over the world, and we mowed down waves of men holding machine guns in *Contra,* that not-so-subtle nod to the action flicks of the '80s starring Stallone and Schwarzenegger, which Thomas and I were watching any time we weren't playing Nintendo.

By my senior year, when I began to skip school at least once a week in the hope I wouldn't have to go to college, I had played through all the games I owned so many times I knew them like my breath, but my breath occasionally choked up inside me, so I found comfort in *Castlevania,* courage in *Contra.* I played *Punch-Out!!* again and again, beating the living hell out of Soda Popinski and Mr. Sandman, until both were battered and bruised. I didn't realize at the time I was hurting, and wanted to hurt someone else. I had no idea what to do with my life, not where to go or what to be. There was something dreadful about the time itself: the trickle-down hope, the savings and loan scandals, the concerts that put forth the belief the world could be saved by music, along with a generous infusion of money. The embarrassing way everyone's bodies were changing, the shifts in tone and the timbre of our voices, the way anger often came flailing out of our acne-clogged pores. Even being middle class was embarrassing for a boy who wanted to save the world.

I didn't realize at the time the characters were caricatures. Despite the sci-fi or fantasy aspect of the games, they mirrored real life: there was always some conflict alive in the world, always some plot to control more land or money, to cleanse an entire ethnicity, to resurrect the ideas of hatred and misunderstanding. Soda Popinski represented an Americanized idea of a Soviet, a cartoon cutout we could ridicule. In the way of the '80s, he was an idea of a person, and not a person himself, the same way so many of us saw the Soviets as one big pink mass on the maps of our social studies classrooms. It only came to me years later that the United States was Super Macho Man: loud, brash, believing himself beautiful. And I realized Macho Man had the same moves as Soda Popinski, only one was left-handed and one right-handed, two sides of the same coin. Both were big and full of bravado. Soda does a little dance; Macho

Man flexes his pecs. I'd say the Japanese creators of the game punked both sides, but we didn't get the joke. We didn't see ourselves in Super Macho Man because we never turned the lens toward us, always aiming it outward.

It also didn't occur to me that I liked controlling others because I couldn't control anything around me. By the time I joined the military late in 1989, I could run through the *Legend of Zelda* untouched by any enemy, as if all a man had to do to stay alive was keep repeating the same set of actions because the reactions of the monsters were set as well. The playlist never changed, and all we had to do was memorize their maneuvers, because they would continue doing the same thing, again and again.

When the Gulf War began my freshman year of college, I was deeply immersed in *Final Fantasy*. I had joined the military because I was tired of being afraid, but with a war looming on the horizon and the very real possibility of fighting, I preferred a war of the digital kind.

My National Guard unit was never activated. We had recently been restructured, and not enough of our soldiers were qualified to pick Soviet-made MIG fighters out of the sky. My stepfather's unit was. He left in October for Fort Sill, and on a rainy Saturday in late November, with all the leaves stripped from the trees, my mother and I drove five hours to see him before he shipped out. When we got home that Sunday I drove back to school, stopping only at the video store to pick out a game that might keep my mind off the impending war, deciding on *Final Fantasy* because, even though the gameplay included fighting, the swords and shields were far enough removed from bullets and bombs that I wouldn't be triggered playing it.

By the time my stepfather arrived in Saudi Arabia, there were hundreds of thousands of soldiers there, and we knew the mother of all wars was coming because we heard about it every night on CNN. Back in my dorm room, I created my adventuring party on the game's opening screen: fighter, thief, black mage, and white mage. There was something about a prophecy. Four warriors arrive, each holding an orb. They go out into a world full of darkness to bring back the light, the same story the media was putting forth about American soldiers sent to the Middle East. In many ways it's the same old story: evil must be vanquished by warriors of virtue.

In other ways it was a new world, both in war and video games. Desert Storm would mark the first time a war had twenty-four-hour news coverage, and it would introduce us all to the smart bomb, FLIR radar, and the Patriot missile. *Final Fantasy* was one of the first turn-based games. Where in many earlier games the fighting consisted of mad button pushing, in *Final Fantasy,* the player gives his party commands: fight, magic, drink, item, run. The party then responds to the commands, the fighters fighting, the mages using magic, occasionally fleeing from enemies too powerful to kill.

All through the last days of November, I played the game, powering up my party. Through finals and the last few days in the dorms, knowing I'd have to report my failing grades to a mother who sat alone at night hoping her husband half a world away hadn't been killed. Through Christmas break, and the cold first days of January, until I drove back to school for my final semester before being kicked out. That spring I spent so much time watching the war, or forgetting about it with video games, I missed too many classes to continue. At the end of the semester, right around the time the troops were coming home, I would receive an academic suspension, and for a while I contemplated joining the army full-time, or suicide if that didn't work out.

When I wasn't playing *Final Fantasy*, my roommate and I watched *GI Joe* and *Transformers* cartoons. It was easier than watching the war, though most every night we did that too, after driving to the liquor store and buying a fifth. We sat in our room and got swimming drunk in front of the TV, waiting. I was always waiting: for the war to begin, for the hammer to fall, to be kicked out of college and so go on with the next part of my life.

In January, after the deadline for Iraq to withdraw from Kuwait had passed, life would again imitate art, or at least video games, like the narrative of *Final Fantasy*. President Bush would give the command to fight, and our army would attack, with magic at first, airplanes the Iraqi army couldn't even detect, Tomahawk missiles they couldn't stop with a shield the size of the Suez Canal. For over a month the bombs fell on Iraq, ripping apart their infrastructure, destroying their communications, their air force, and their will to fight. It was a strategic dismantling of an army, a systematic destruction on a level we'd never seen before, one I can't compare to any video game, unless it was to be reminded of the flattened cities in *Missile Command* after the missiles came too fast and my puny defenses couldn't keep them out.

In February the ground force went in. In less than a hundred hours they swept clean the desert. Apache helicopters and A-10 Warthogs cleared the few tanks that had survived the falling bombs. The Iraqi army surrendered in the tens of thousands, deciding that they could neither fight nor flee. Hussein had his men set fire to the oil wells, which burned for months, spewing oily flames that reminded me of sulfur, as if hell had come.

By the time the war ended, I had finished *Final Fantasy*, defeating the final enemy, whose name, if I remember correctly, was Chaos. This was only after I had defeated the four orb elementals, dragons, kraken, and other mythological creatures like those the Bible says will appear in the last days. After vanquishing Chaos, we learn that the Light Warriors have been stuck in a time-loop and have been fighting the same battle for thousands of years. The text tells us to never forget the good and true, but in the blackness of the final screen, I hit start again, and began a new game. I chose different characters this time, a thief and a monk and a red mage, but knew the gameplay would be the same. Still, late at night in my dorm room, I needed some screen to keep from seeing the silence inside me. The war had ended, but I knew there would be another one. There always was. On the cartoons we watched, Cobra was always trying to conquer the world, and only G.I. Joe was there to stop him. The Decepticons were always trying to destroy the Autobots. On the games I played, warriors of light were always trying to keep back the darkness, but the world was much more complex than video games made it out to be. The one truth they held onto was that the past would always circle back to the present.

In the years after I dropped out of college, when I was working odd jobs and then making a second and third attempt at a degree, came the Super Nintendo. I played it all through the '90s, though most of the games I liked best were reboots of the classics, because we always want to be back where we once were, even if we were scared and alone, because that familiar fear is easier to face than the future.

The *Legend of Zelda* had been rebooted, and so had *Metroid*, now named *Super Metroid*. Both games had bigger and badder bosses and better graphics, but the storylines were the same. Zelda had been kidnapped again. The metroids were back, having multiplied, driven by the Mother Brain, which Samus once again destroys.

In 1993 I made another attempt at college. I lived in a little apartment near campus and drank too much playing the old games. The Gulf War had ended victoriously, but I felt like we'd all been duped, that the war was little more than a chance to flex our might in the Middle East. I had grown out of my teen idealism and was questioning my military service, so I sat in the dark of my apartment playing *Street Fighter II* and *Contra III*, numbing myself with alcohol and video games to the point that some nights I contemplated jumping off the Arkansas River bridge near Nuclear One, a power plant that sent great gouts of steam skyward and forced me to consider how quickly we'd all die if it ever melted down.

At my weekend National Guard drills, we played wargames. Late at night I monitored the radio for enemy movement or lay prone in the rain alongside an empty base road watching for convoys, wondering what the hell we were doing. I wanted answers, but no one cared to ask any questions. I wanted to know what we had accomplished. I was old enough to understand that all war comes with a price, but the number of dead American soldiers was so low in comparison to the numbers sent it seemed we all accepted that their sacrifice served the greater good, only no one was asking what the greater good was.

So we played Super Nintendo. With his income tax return money, Thomas bought a Sega, even though we couldn't afford to eat anything other than ramen noodles. Days we were supposed to be in class, we played *Columns,* a *Tetris* rip-off that had us stacking colored gems, to what end I don't know, except a higher score than our opponent. On weekends we played Spades with the two girls who lived next door, trying every time to talk them into strip poker, a fact I'm not proud of, even when I remind myself how little self-worth I felt then. We watched reruns of *Star Trek* and wondered what it would be like cruising through the universe seeing space unfold on the video screen, backed by the firepower of photon torpedoes. We wondered about the energizer, and if it could send us anywhere we wanted, perhaps to a time we weren't afraid, although I don't know when that might have been.

At the end of the spring semester in 1994, I dropped out of college again and moved back home with my parents, where I slept eighteen hours a day and woke only to stare at the screensaver on my computer monitor. Sometimes I booted up *BattleTech* or turned on my Nintendo long enough to save a princess. I had started writing and was working on a novel, but the difficulty of forming my thoughts into sentences that made sense seemed as hard as saving the world. I was still going to National Guard drills once a month but had suddenly realized I could quit. I had once thought I would be a life-long soldier, but now, in the mid-90s, at age twenty-three, I had begun to wonder what the constant threat of war was doing to me. It seemed I'd been at war all my life, from the Cold War to the Gulf War, and the only escape from it I could find came from games like *Missile Command* and *MechWarrior,* not really an escape at all.

So in August of 1995, five years to the day since Hussein had invaded Kuwait, I left the military. I had never been able to shake the scenes CNN showed of bombs falling on Baghdad. I had never been able to rid myself of the images beamed back to us of tanks caught in the crosshairs of our night vision lenses, of Tomahawk missiles lifting off from the decks of US aircraft carriers. Of the technological reports of our smart bombs and how they could strike a radio station without touching the school next door, of the advancements of Stealth fighters and Multiple Launch Rocket Systems, all announced with the same sort of superiority I felt when my BattleMech rolled onto the field strapped with machine guns and missiles. Of SCUD missiles falling on Tel Aviv, and US-made Patriots shooting them out of the sky just like in *Missile Command*.

Not long after I left the military, a friend bought a PlayStation, and when I went to his house to get stoned on Saturday night we played *Diablo*, a game in which we had to destroy the ultimate evil of Satan. Around this same time, my friends and I started playing *Dungeons & Dragons*. We all worked second shift at a toy factory, and when we got off near midnight we drove to the liquor store, then settled into a world of elves and wizards and whiskey, sometimes playing until morning, when we'd stumble home and sleep until time for work. Caught up in distracting ourselves with quests, we rarely wondered what we were doing, which was the way we wanted it. It's easier to accept fiction than truth, easier to walk through a world of dragons and never think about the dungeons we create for ourselves.

By the time I managed to finish college and started grad school, I had graduated to Xbox. I was writing in the morning and taking classes at night, and when I got home my daughters were asleep, so I played video games until the worry I was carrying around with me went away. My daughters had both been born while I was trying to find my way in the world, kicking around from job to job, finally following my desire to tell stories. There seemed nothing else to do. I didn't want to work in the factories or the fast-food places I had been working in, so another attempt at a degree seemed the only option.

A month after my family moved to North Carolina, four airplanes were hijacked in the sky. Two of them, in moments immortalized ever after, flew into the World Trade Center Twin Towers. I had turned on the TV just as the second one struck. We all sat stunned, sure the world had just changed forever. Later we would learn fighters had been scrambled from Langley, but like in *Missile Command* when the missiles started flying too fast, they did not make it in time to intercept the airplanes, and I still wonder, if they'd made it in time, if the fighter pilots would have been given the order to shoot down the stolen planes.

In the fallout, I bought an Xbox. As the Patriot Act was passed and airport security tightened, I felt at times like I had an invisible noose around my neck. US forces invaded Afghanistan, just as the Soviet Union had done two decades earlier. In the way of empire, we had bases in countries on every corner and military operations everywhere, and it never occurred to us to ask if what we were doing was right.

So I played *MechAssault*, released in 2002, a reboot of the old *MechWarrior* game we'd played in Coach Bailey's computer class, which seemed a world ago. The Cold War was over, the Gulf War was over, but now there was another war, one that we all knew would last forever. When I put my daughters to sleep, I stayed awake late into the night running through the campaign, whose story consisted of a religious cult turned to terrorism. In my giant Battle Mech, I stomped on little fleeing fanatics. I'm ashamed of the joy it gave me to shoot them with machine guns that fired bullets so big their bodies simply vanished, but I was thinking of the plane that struck the South Tower, still projecting hatred, finding catharsis in destruction.

After *MechAssault*, I played *Morrowind*, a game that drops your character into a small village with no idea of who you are or how you got there. There's little in the way of tutorial. I often

MISSILE COMMAND  ·  107

wondered, seeing on the news the nightly explosions in Kabul and Kandahar, how we got to where we were. President Bush and Vice President Cheney were turning their hoary eyes on Iraq, and though I could trace the history of the Middle East, how most of the territorial lines were drawn on a map in the aftermath of World War II, with little regard for the people who lived there, I couldn't see how that had gotten us to where we were, forgetting, even as I played games I played in junior high, that each war is simply a reboot of an old one. World War I was a replay of the German invasion of France in 1870, World War II was a replay of World War I, and both the Korean and Vietnam Wars came out of the ashes of World War II. It made sense, in that light, that we would go back to Iraq, that we'd try to succeed in Afghanistan where the Soviet Union failed.

When I graduated, I got a job teaching how to form words into arguments, but I was still forming my arguments in silence. The levels of the new *Castlevania* game reminded me there's always evil in the world. *MechAssault* meant that we would keep building weapons until there was little distinction between weapon and person, as if all our weapons are only manifestations of what we wished we could be: machine guns on our shoulders, missiles on our backs, enough armor to allow us to walk into enemy fire and escape unscathed. Even then, I didn't yet understand that we too often feel small. To fight that feeling, some of us use words. Others use weapons, but both reactions come from the same fear.

In 2006, with the war in Afghanistan entering its fifth year, my wife bought me *World of Warcraft* for Christmas. I had switched back to computer games, *Baldur's Gate* and *Neverwinter Nights*, and *Warcraft's* immersive world hooked me the minute I installed it on my computer. I played late at night when my daughters went to sleep, and for a time, I didn't have to worry about them. I didn't have to worry about the world they were growing up in. Every night we heard on the news about IEDs and insurgents. For three years we'd been in Iraq as well, after a campaign called Shock and Awe, meant to ensure a quick victory, but the war had slowly settled into the same kind of war as in Afghanistan.

So it made sense to immerse myself once again in a world of war, since we lived in one. We had always lived in one. My stepfather fought in Desert Storm, a war I narrowly avoided in the same way my father narrowly avoided Vietnam. My grandfather fought in World War II and Korea. My daughters were born just before the US invaded Afghanistan; they entered adulthood with US forces still there. I suspect we will be there always, the same way we still have bases in Germany and Japan.

In *Warcraft* I chose as my character a rogue because of an ability called stealth. I suppose I wanted to walk unseen through the world. I chose a female rogue because my daughters were beside me when I created her on the character screen, and maybe I wanted my daughters to be able to walk through the world unseen by any monsters, or men. To be able to vanish, another ability the rogue has, when any danger came near. They watched over my shoulder as I steered my rogue through the streets of Stormwind, as I stealthed through the Deadmines and Deadwind Pass.

As they got older, they began to play games of their own. Some nights I booted up my Xbox and we played *Dungeons & Dragons: Heroes* together, or I dug the Nintendo out of the closet to play *Gauntlet*, a reboot of an old game but one that still had the goal of getting out alive. They played the old *Zelda* games, and I surprised myself when I remembered where the hidden items were: the blue ring and red ring, the master sword and silver arrow.

When I grew tired of *Warcraft*, I played *Rift*, a game in which rifts open everywhere, all over the world, and monsters pour through. At any time, any place, any moment in the world, a rift can open up, and armies step out, ready to kill and conquer, and that felt true. After *Rift* I played *Star Wars: The Old Republic*, a game that, like the movies, claims to be in the past but uses weapons from the future, as if, once again, the past and future are the same.

I say they are. My daughters are now gone into the world, but I still press buttons every morning, trying to make some sense of the world. At night I play *Destiny 2*, in which my character has superpowers bestowed upon her by a great god-like thing in the sky. These Guardians carry machine guns and hand cannons, and they fight the forces of evil in the universe. It's comforting to know that I am fighting for the good of all mankind. It's comforting to know there are no consequences if I lose. My character can be resurrected if killed, and all I have to do if the world ends is reboot the game, keep pressing buttons until I find an outcome that I like.

I keep trying. Because I don't want to feel helpless. Because I'm scared of the men who make the decisions, who believe war is little more than a game. Because I grew up with games that always gave me another chance. Because, like the men monitoring the skies, like all of us who watched the nightly news, I grew up behind a screen. Like so many of us now, our faces bathed in computer light late at night, trying to find connections, scrolling through stories for some semblance of hope, some reassurance that there's a way to win, to save the world from ourselves.

# Morgue

The day we found the morgue, Dee said we were all going to die. At the time we lived on the grounds of an old tuberculosis sanatorium, where we obsessed over death. This was 1981, and most of the buildings were boarded over. What few remained open had been converted to homes for individuals with intellectual disabilities, which meant that all day, while we looked out the windows of our houses, we saw the residents walking around the manicured lawns, and all night, as we tried to dream ourselves elsewhere, we heard them calling to one another, seemingly like ghosts.

The whole place was haunted. It had been built a few years before World War I, when tuberculosis was ravaging the country. After the war, the first buildings filled with soldiers who caught TB in the trenches. For twenty years they wasted away in little rooms staring out the windows. In 1941, around the time bombs were falling on Pearl Harbor, the Nyberg was built, a hospital that seemed to us in the early '80s like it was a half a mile long. By then another war was going on, this one in the air above our heads, and we called it Cold. Missiles and transmissions were flying over us at all times, and at any time, we thought, they could come crashing down.

Maybe this morbidity was why we went to the morgue. We had heard rumors that nuclear missile silos were housed beneath the hill, and though I don't recall whether it was all the bombs we saw on the nightly news or the buildings themselves that caused us to believe such a thing, I do recall that around Christmas, maintenance put a giant Star of Bethlehem atop the Nyberg, like a signal we should follow, so maybe we thought we would find beneath Bethlehem something that would save us. I'd say now we were only kids, exploring our world like kids everywhere, only our backyard was an old sanatorium instead of a suburb. Instead of bake sales, we had boarded over buildings, and instead of Boy Scout meetings, we sought out the old morgue, beneath which nuclear missiles were said to be waiting.

From our houses we crossed a small creek and went over a dew-wet field behind Dorm One, Dee leading, with Brock behind my brother and me. There were four dorms, but only One and Two were still open. The others stood like stones, windows blacked out by boards, shutters sagging or gone altogether. Past Dorm One we crouched in the shadows of the pine trees until the coast was clear, then we crossed the street running in front of the Nyberg and washed up against its walls.

Dee, whose uncle worked maintenance at the institute, said the door to the morgue was never locked. Still hugging the stone side of the old building, we ducked beneath the overhang where hearses used to dock to bring out the dead in the tuberculosis days. The door was indeed unlocked. Dee turned the handle. We waited in the darkness for our eyes to adjust, and I'll say now I was more than a little scared, though I don't remember if I was scared of what we might find or of getting into trouble.

A long hall led to an antechamber where faint light gathered sourceless around us. Already, Brock, a year younger than we were, which meant he was eight or nine at the time, wanted to go home. I'll say I did too. Old equipment stood everywhere: tables and gurneys and steel sinks unstuck from the walls. A metal bed with wooden legs tied on it. In one corner, crumbled tiles that had fallen from some other ceiling.

Spraypainted on the walls were the words of old lovers proclaiming themselves forever together. Cigarette butts and beer bottles said we weren't the first to come here since it had closed. Most of the doors had been removed, and a cold wind whipped down the halls, and the building above us moaned as if it held within the spirits of those who had once walked here.

I don't remember how long we rummaged through the rooms or what we were looking for, but I do remember finding storage coolers that had once held corpses, and drainage tubes for embalming. Old cabinets full of brown bottles meant to preserve bodies. Machinery more medieval than medicinal. Long silver implements Brock said were to pull out brains and other body parts, so I suppose we were seeking death in the way morbid curiosity surrounds kids still coming to terms with life. All our understanding comes from discovery, even if our findings are forged out of fear.

After sifting through the discarded debris, we saw at the back of the morgue a sign that said Bomb Shelter. I still don't know if there was a separate bomb shelter in the building, or if the sign meant the morgue was where we should go if the war began, but we knew upon seeing it that the threat we'd heard about was real. There may not have been a missile silo beneath our shoes, but the Cold War was as real as the morgue, as cold as the bodies of those once embalmed here. I was terrified of fire, and it came to me then that here was where we would hide if the bombs ever fell, under a building where thousands had died with disease in their lungs, unable to breath, in a room where their blood was drained through tubes and their bodies embalmed so they could be buried.

"We're all going to die," Dee said, voice pitched like a late-night murder movie, and we all laughed, though I saw more than one lingering look back at the sign and the silver implements and the spray-painted names, as if we would remember it all forever.

It was cold when we came out. The dark was starting to set in. A line of cars was heading down the hill with their headlights on, like a funeral procession, and standing in the light of the Star of Bethlehem, I saw the leaves on the trees lifting in the first hint of wind.

That night a storm came up out of the west. A warm front had moved in to clash with winter's cold, and on the TV, weather warnings lit up the state of Arkansas like radiation. As the wind started to rise, my mother took us to my grandfather's storm shelter, where we sat in a little room beneath the earth in the light of a kerosene lamp while the storm shook above us. All through the night, our shadows stood on the walls. Each crash of thunder convinced me something was coming, so to soothe my shaking, my grandmother sang some silly song, her old hands rubbing the small of my back. I can still feel it there, soothing away all the scared. I never told her about the morgue and the bomb shelter and how scared I was sometimes, but I think she knew in the same way she always carried around some unnamed worry with her.

Twenty years later, when my daughters were little, they often woke crying. A spring storm would come up sudden as the end of the earth, and they'd flinch in each flash of thunder. I sometimes rocked them to sleep while watching the nightly news. I listened to George W. Bush say the world was either for us or against us, and some nights, when everything seemed to be circling back to bomb shelters, I stayed awake wondering how anyone could sleep. We were living in a basement apartment then, and when my daughters woke in the night, I sang to them some silly song.

Forty years after the morgue, I live in the Midwest, in a city where a movie about the end of the world was once filmed. I sleep in the basement when storms come out of the west, and flinch at each flash of thunder. The wars are still everywhere. In 2019 the US pulled out of the Intermediate-Range Nuclear Forces Treaty, which had stood for over thirty years. Russia followed suit, and within three days, both countries had fired missiles into the sky, like a warning, or a sign. Sometimes I wake in the middle of the night, wishing for a song to soothe me back to sleep. The basement is cold as a morgue, and I sit there in the darkness until the storm moves off, until I can breathe again, until I'm certain I won't be buried.

# Step on a Crack

I still won't step on cracks so I don't break my mother's back. I still think the last one there is a rotten egg, that if I make a face too many times it'll freeze that way, that if I find a penny and pick it up, then all day long I'll have good luck.

I still believe you're only safe when you're touching home base, and I still cross my fingers to make something untrue. I still knock on wood to ward off bad luck, and I still hide under the covers some days in hopes the monsters won't find me.

An apple a day keeps the doctor away, but that only relates to diet. There's no superstition to keep the body safe, unless we count the covers over our heads, or how we have to change our faces so they don't freeze in fear. When a hearse passes by, I pull over to the side of the road, although maybe that's out of respect rather than superstition.

I only know that some days I have to pull over when the news comes on the radio and I'm reminded of all the things we believed as children: that monsters only come out at night, that the slowest among us would suffer some punishment, that there was such a thing as safe. We thought as children of the '80s that all the danger came from the sky, but even then we knew you couldn't dodge bullets, back when we formed our small fingers into handguns and aimed them at one another. Sometimes we used rocks or sticks, and sometimes we said we had shields, but despite the strange superstitions we subscribed to, we always knew we couldn't sidestep or shield ourselves, though we claimed to every time someone shot at us, scared as we were of dying. We always knew there was no getting up. That once we were hit, we were out of the game, stuck there in the dirt with the others already shot.

We can check the closet and beneath the bed, but monsters are never where we expect them to be. I never say "cross my heart and hope to die" anymore, nor do I wish a thousand needles in my eye. I never say "Bloody Mary" in front of a mirror and I never say "one, two, Freddy's coming for you," like in that old movie about a man killing kids, because the screams at schools are no longer laughter, the coverage on our computer screens more terrible than anything we ever imagined.

Growing up I always believed the world would end in the kind of fire that came from missiles, not machine guns. But I still believe blowing out candles grants a wish, so on my daughter's next birthday I'll whisper in her ear what to wish for. Then I'll give her a rabbit's foot. I'll search for four-leaf clovers. A horseshoe, a ladybug, the number seven sewn big over her shirt with bulletproof thread.

Because everything we learned as children was true. We know that parents can die from breaking if their children stand in the wrong spot. We know sticks and stones and broken bones hurt worse than words ever could, with the exception of "There's been a shooting at your son's school." We know the monsters are everywhere, and we know there's no place to hide that they can't find you.

# When Buckwheat Got Shot

Late one Saturday night, cross-legged on the sea-green carpet before the old Magnavox, with smoke eddying above me from my mother's cigarette, I watched a man murdered on national TV. In a breaking special report, an actor pretending to be Ted Koppel tells us that Buckwheat, the once-beloved child actor from the Little Rascals, has been shot. He had just left the *Saturday Night Live* studios in New York when an unknown assailant pulled a handgun and shot him several times. In the recorded clip Koppel plays, Buckwheat's body jerks with the impact of the bullets. His eyes go wide, and he falls back against the car while several of his bodyguards swarm the shooter.

Buckwheat's other bodyguards push him into the car, and the car speeds off. In the studio, Koppel tells us again that Buckwheat has been shot, that America is stunned. An infographic spins onto the screen showing Buckwheat being shot. Below the graphic runs the tagline: "The Shooting of Buckwheat: America Stunned." A few moments later, the cameras are at the hospital. Alfalfa stands in the corridor saying, "I can't believe it." Koppel asks Alfalfa if he's seen the video, then shows him the clip. When the camera goes into the operating room, where Buckwheat's life hangs by a thread, Koppel asks the doctor if he's seen the video, then shows him the clip.

Each time the broadcast takes a short break, the infographic reappears. "America Waits and Worries" comes after "America Stunned," then, finally, changes to "America Mourns." The infographics are sponsored by Texxon, a fictitious combination of Texaco and Exxon whose motto is "Life Goes On." After the announcement that Buckwheat has died, the advertisement reads, "Life goes on because Buckwheat would have wanted it that way." In classic comedy fashion, Koppel, played by Joe Piscopo, goes back to the clip again, and again we see Buckwheat being shot. This time the video is slowed. Koppel/Piscopo tries to analyze where the shots are coming from and who the shooter is, as Buckwheat's body jerks, his eyes go wide, and he falls again against the car.

The broadcast ends with a tribute to Buckwheat, starting with a picture of the actual Buckwheat from *The Little Rascals,* then changing to Eddie Murphy playing the character he created. The final image, of course, is one of Buckwheat being shot. I won't bother to tell you how many times Koppel repeats that Buckwheat has been shot during the six minutes of coverage, or the number of times he shows the shooting, but believe me when I say it comes close to repeating itself so often it ceases to be funny, passing whatever invisible barrier demarcates how many times we'll laugh at a thing.

At school that Monday, all my friends were still laughing about it. We kept asking each other if we'd seen the video of Buckwheat being shot, because that was the repeated point of the skit, even if we didn't understand what it was asking of us or know then how many times we would watch and rewatch the infamous moments of our lives, the ones that move us to some place we've never been.

We didn't understand context at the time. We knew Reagan had been shot two years earlier, but we didn't know the Buckwheat skit was a commentary on the way the media covered the assassination attempt. We had heard about JFK in Dallas, but we didn't know about MLK or RFK or Malcolm X. Nor did we know that, years later, those who grew up with such images in their heads would continue to replay them more times than fictional Koppel showed Buckwheat's shooting. My father, nineteen at the time and fearing the draft, had seen a Vietnamese man murdered on the nightly news. My mother remembered pictures of the little Vietnamese girl running down the street with napalm burning her naked body, her mouth open in a silent scream. My grandfather, born long before TV came into our homes, remembered the headlines of Pearl Harbor.

A few years after Buckwheat was shot on live TV, the Space Shuttle *Challenger* would explode midflight. I was in PE when it launched, and we had all crowded into the coach's office to watch it on the tiny TV. I can still recall the collective gasp, and some girl whose name I can't remember moaning "Oh, no" again and again. That evening the nightly news ran a short clip of Christa McAuliffe and the astronauts waving as they walked out to board the shuttle, then replayed the Challenger breaking apart, a clip we would see again and again over the next few days. An image of the explosion would appear on the covers of *Time* and *Newsweek* and every major newspaper in the country, working itself into our collective conscious.

My senior year of high school, we would stand and cheer when the Berlin Wall began to crumble, banishing the bogeymen we'd long thought the Soviets to be, but during my second semester of college, new bogeymen would appear to take their place, and bombs began to fall on Baghdad after a long buildup. Still captivated by what I saw on the screen, I watched CNN every night, the only difference being I was old enough now to calm my fears with depressing amounts of alcohol. I can still recall the clippings I cut from the newspaper and posted on my bulletin board: A-10 Warthogs and Apache helicopters and Tomahawk missiles firing from the decks of battleships in the Red Sea, armored tanks rolling across the desert toward Baghdad, oil fires burning into the desert night.

In 1995 we saw the ripped-off face of the federal building in Oklahoma City. In 1996, at a concert celebrating the Olympics in Atlanta, there came a blast in the background that sent a shockwave rippling through all of us. I've watched the video of the airplanes striking the Twin Towers more times than I care to count, seen the shock and awe over Baghdad that signaled the beginning to another war so many times it seems as if, every time an explosion rocks the screen, I shake inside. At the Columbine school shooting, security cameras caught the shooters as they herded kids into the cafeteria, and I'm waiting, any day now, for video of children being shot that we'll watch again and again and again, until there's nothing left inside us, not even hope.

One semester, a former soldier in a college class I taught showed a video of his unit engaged in a firefight. This was real footage, he said. He had shot it himself with a helmet camera. These were real soldiers in a real battle with real bullets. He kept repeating the word *real* as if to distinguish it from what we see on TV or the internet, and I think he only meant that he experienced it himself, that he was not removed from the action and hidden behind a screen, but I kept wondering if there was any difference. Sometimes it feels like we're living in a documentary that looks more like a dark comedy, because we can see these shows any time of day, anywhere in the world: a bomb or a bullet or someone like Buckwheat, standing on a city street waiting for a car to carry him home.

The week after Buckwheat was shot, his assassin, a man named John David Stutts, was shot in the same way Lee Harvey Oswald was shot by Jack Ruby. Stutts was also played by Eddie Murphy, and we all watched it and talked about it that Monday in the halls of our high school or on the factory floor or by the water cooler in the anonymous office buildings we already saw ourselves working in, but I say now that we didn't laugh as hard or, if we did, we had to force it. That somehow we knew the writers would keep coming back to the same old gag, repeating it ad infinitum: the shooter is shot, and then that shooter is shot, and then even that shooter is shot, like replaying the same moments over and over, trying to make some sense of them. As if we're always stunned by what we see, always waiting and worrying, always, over and over and over again, in mourning.

# Red Shirt Guy Is Going to Die

From the captain's chair, Kirk makes the decision to beam down. He carries as crew the guy in the red shirt, who is going to die. You know it, I know it, Captain Kirk knows it, because we've all seen it seventy times. It's the only reason he's here. Neither Kirk nor Spock nor Bones McCoy can die, so it has to be Red Shirt Guy. He'll be choked by an evil android or eaten by an alien species. He'll be killed by a Klingon. He'll be thrown down a mine shaft, and the main characters will shake their heads sadly for a moment before moving on.

In the *Star Wars* world, the stormtroopers are going to die. Lots of them are. That's why we get so many scenes of vast formations, men standing at attention while the Emperor inspects them. They're going to fire endlessly and hit nothing, but when Han Solo or Princess Leia fires back, stormtroopers are going to die. They'll fall down an air shaft in the Death Star. They will spin into space when their TIE fighter catches fire, then crash into a planet with a little puff of smoke, but despite the ones that die, their numbers will hardly be diminished.

That X-wing fighter guy is going to die too. If we don't know his name, other than "Red Five," he's going to die. He's going to smash into a star destroyer or be shot by the tower cannons on the Death Star. He'll die a fiery, screaming death, and none of us will care for more than a second because we didn't know his name.

That cowboy is going to die. That peasant is going to die. They are extras. And during the gun fights and sword fights, extras have to die so we can understand how important it is for the heroes to win. Red Shirt Guy dying shows us the deadliness of the planet Kirk has beamed down to, and why he must subdue it. Stormtroopers dying reminds us the Empire can always throw more men at its enemies.

As a child I imagined myself like Captain Kirk or Luke Skywalker. I sat in the big chair of the USS *Enterprise* as we sped through space watching worlds whip past on the giant screen. Spock was my best friend and taught me the Vulcan nerve pinch. I trained under Yoda, learning backflips and force-pulls. I didn't realize Klingons were caricatures of Soviet soldiers. That the evil Galactic Empire represented any government that relied on totalitarianism to expand its dominion.

Yet, for Halloween one year, I costumed as a stormtrooper. With my plastic helmet on, no one knew who I was. We all wore masks: goblins and ghouls and minions of greater monsters, children who grew up in front of giant screens trying to emulate what we'd seen. We were werewolves and witches, creatures with more power than we could command, but none of us could name why we wanted to be something else.

Every time I go to the movies, I see men my age leaned forward as if invested in the outcome, but a century of popular cinema has taught us nothing. We've always aligned ourselves with the heroes, but when the projector stops rolling and the lights come on, we blink in the sudden illumination, drawn back inside ourselves. In the morning we'll drive to work through rush-hour traffic and enter our cubicles like any number of others around us, stare at our screens as if we were plotting courses across the galaxy or planning attacks in the coming war, never acknowledging what the movies never mention, that our world only needs saving from itself.

In the movies, the stormtroopers are sent in to seal the latest threat but never stop to wonder who's voicing the commands. Red Shirt Guy goes out to investigate but never makes his report—his body is found, the cause of death mysterious, and only the audience knows the Klingons killed him. In war terms, we would call these characters cannon fodder: men who must die to keep more important men alive. In the cubicles and cramped apartments, the tract homes in the sprawling suburbs, we watch the Red Shirts get killed and call it entertainment.

Suppose their deaths were preventable. The Galactic Empire realizes the value of stormtroopers and gives up its hope of universal domination. Red Shirt Guy suddenly understands the Klingons are caricatures. He explains he's tired of fighting an unending proxy war on planets he'll never return to. The peasants overthrow the strict caste system of ancient Japan and melt all the swords into ploughshares. The cowboys realize they are fighting over land that none of them will ever own and so ride off into the sunset without shooting anybody.

I'd like to be a Red Shirt, wandering the bowels of the *Starship Enterprise*. Or a stormtrooper stationed on the Death Star. Not the guy who fires the planet-destroying laser, but some low-level administrator, maybe the guy who oversees the secret trench. I imagine those guys are more like me and you, there on the lower floors in our well-fitted uniforms, while above us men in gray suits make decisions about where we will go. They decide who beams down to the planet, who dies on the front lines. Who destroys the world, while the rest of are staring at a screen.

# The Other Place

Because the Baptist minister said so often I'd die by fire, I was convinced missiles would soon fall from the sky. This was the early '80s, and when the preacher stood at the pulpit and said all our days would come to a fiery end, I imagined the ICBMs of the Soviet Union. We stood at the height of the Cold War, and some summer nights with heat lightning on the horizon, I was sure the missiles were coming and soon the wave would wash over us, bringing a brief white light that heralded forever.

On Sundays the sermon was always about fire. Some Wednesday services, the preacher relented and related the love of Jesus Christ, but on Sundays, with the pews full and people needing to be reminded why they were there, he went back to fire and brimstone, claiming that sin would send us to the lake of sulfur. In my mind, I imagined not some hell inside the earth, but burning cities, and because the war was cold, the fire would be as well. I'd read, even at that age, how scientists theorized the smoke from the fires of nuclear war would obscure the sun, bringing about a nuclear winter, a phrase that made as much sense to me as Cold War.

So, sitting in the pews as the preacher told us that a thousand years was only the first tick of eternity's clock, I imagined waves and waves of terrible cold washing over us. I imagined the eternal pit burned so hot it had crossed over to cold. We were told all the time to believe things that stood in stark opposition to each other: that we fought for peace or that our country's greatest war was civil, so believing fire could be cold came as easily as believing that God was both vengeful and forgiving.

When he wasn't telling us of the terrible heat of hell, the preacher sometimes described the last hour of humanity. He seemed angry as he told us how the Four Horsemen would come riding down out of the sky and let loose a thousand years of darkness and destruction. War would engulf the world. Death would reign on his white horse, and finally, God would turn his back on all those who did not worship him, leading me back to that thought about vengeance and forgiveness.

When the time came for the invitation, I was shivering. I don't know now whether from fear or cold. We had just learned God was an angry and vengeful God who couldn't wait to destroy this sinful earth, and now we were told, like a late-night '80s infomercial, that all we had to do to save ourselves from sin was to walk down to the front. Then we would rise to heaven when the last days came, but all I could think about was how cold it would be way up in the clouds.

We were still a few years away from President Reagan's proposal to put lasers in space, but I knew from reading *Time* in the town library that when the ICBMs were fired, they would arc into outer space and then descend from on high, like stars falling from heaven. If God wanted to stop them, he could, I theorized, with a swat of His cosmic hand, but He preferred—according to the preacher—to let the last days play out like prophecy.

That prophecy seemed at hand. For most of the '70s, the US and the Soviet Union had been working on cordial communications, but the 1979 Soviet Invasion of Afghanistan and the subsequent elections of Ronald Reagan and Margaret Thatcher had changed the West's policy. Now the US seemed more interested in fighting. The US imposed a grain embargo, then began to sell weapons to anti-Soviet forces in Afghanistan.

When Reagan came into power, he started another proxy war, through a policy called rollback, which was a form of regime change through economic means. Reagan didn't believe the Soviet Union's economy could support its war effort, so in an attempt to dismantle the USSR, he continued to build: bombs and bullets, aircraft carriers and the aircraft they carried, Intercontinental Ballistic Missiles (that now held numerous warheads and could strike a dozen different targets).

The Soviets, he theorized, could never keep up. They would try and fail, crashing their economy. But the buildup gave the US and the Soviet Union the two largest militaries the modern world had ever seen, with enough nuclear weapons to end the earth a hundred times. And since Reagan was embraced by the Christian Coalition and the Moral Majority and the religious right, who had opposed the Strategic Arms Limitation Talks, it seemed God was in favor of the end.

If I worried too much about war, it was because I saw it everywhere. In summer, National Guard units from all over the state of Arkansas came to nearby Fort Chaffee. Later, after I joined the military, I would spend several summers on base, but as a kid I knew only the fear we felt at the trembling in the earth that seemed to come from there. On weekends, artillery fell with a sound like thunder, and the ground shook beneath the soles of our shoes. Airplanes streaked overhead faster than their sound, and on some hot August days the fire from the bombs ignited the dry grasses.

Some days, even forty miles away, the world lay thick with smoke. Blackened grass stretched forever, and charred trees smoldered. Driving through the ruins with my father, we could see the white tails of deer fleeing the fires. For years he worked for the Forest Service and fought fires all over the West. When I asked him if flames would ever engulf us all, he said, "Not if I can help it," but looking at the stretches of forest burned by bombs, I didn't quite believe him.

All through summer the artillery rained down and the fires burned, until fall when the soldiers went home. The artillery went silent, and the airplanes flew fewer and fewer missions, as if the war had ended and there was no longer any need to patrol the skies. There were no convoys on the roads, no constant reminders that our country was always waiting for a war.

Only a skeleton crew of civilians stayed on, as if the soldiers had all been shipped somewhere. A few MPs still circled the base looking for kids out joyriding or hunters with no permits, but the artillery stood locked up, barrels pointing at the ground instead of the sky. The Air National Guard sometimes sounded high overhead, but the bombs stopped falling, and with the cold came quiet.

But for me the war was always there, even in winter. Mist rose like smoke from the creeks and ponds. Snow fell in the burned forests, and deer fled from hunters. In the early mornings, gunshots rang out over the countryside, and more than once out walking in the woods, I came across blood drawn on snow and freshly eviscerated guts steaming in the cold.

What I imagined then, in the snow and cold, my breath flowering before me like a memory of some lost world, was that it had all ended. I would imagine that the fire that fell from the sky had obscured the sun and we were living now in the last days of the earth. That we had to hunt to sustain ourselves, and that every blood spill I found meant less food to eat. Soon, I thought, we would be shooting each other.

We heard about the end everywhere. Every morning we held our hands over our hearts and pledged allegiance to the flag, of the United States of America, and to the republic, for which it stands. One nation, and even then we knew the "under God" part was important, a reminder of the enmities that existed in the world. We didn't know "under God" had been added at the onset of the Cold War, but we knew that the atheist communist Soviets didn't believe in God, and we had to hate them because they wanted to destroy us, or take away our freedoms, or both.

After pledging our allegiance, our teacher, Mrs. Butler, whom we called Mrs. Born-Again, led us in prayer, long after the Supreme Court said she couldn't. At church the songs we sang exemplified the times: *I have seen Him in the watchfires of a hundred circling camps* was a favorite line of mine, from a song that praised God's terrible, swift sword. *As He died to make men holy, let us live to make men free* was another, a lyric hearkening back to that war we still called civil. We sang of the blood of Christ. That God was both merciful and mighty. That Christian soldiers were marching onward as to war, carrying the cross of Jesus.

We didn't know the nation had not been founded on the Christian faith as much as faith had been inserted as a bulwark against the Soviets. Prophecy said the final holy war would take place in the Valley of Megiddo in the Middle East, but we knew the Soviet Union would stand against us.

In social studies we learned about communism, which our teacher explained as a system of government founded on the principle of keeping everyone in poverty. No one had free will over there, she said, nodding at the massive pink blob on the map, and everyone worked twenty-hour days for a single crust of bread. The government was corrupt and often sent anyone who disagreed with them to Siberia, another amorphous blob on the map.

The heads of the church felt the same way. Jerry Falwell, leader of the Moral Majority, said the Soviets could not be trusted. That they would enslave us the minute we let down our guard. Only from a position of strength could we negotiate with them, Falwell said in 1981, because they were coming for us.

They were evil, and we were good. Our cause—it didn't matter then that none of us could explain our cause—was just. It also didn't seem to matter to any of the men preaching all this that no matter the cause, the world would end in flames, and that whoever was left standing would have only ashes to rule. Those missiles aimed at the sky were meant to end us, but ours would end them as well, and in the nuclear winter that followed, I imagined those left would be forced to eat each other or something just as awful, so it didn't really matter who we called good or evil if both sides ended up as cannibals.

But adults rarely recognize their own contradictions. It never occurred to anyone at the Baptist church down the road what would happen to a generation raised on hate and fear, the exact things the church was supposed to stand against. Yoda recognized it in 1980 when he said, "Wars not make one great," but it seemed our leaders, then and now, church and state, never knew that. They wanted our aggressions ordained, our sins sanctioned, as long as we aimed them, like missiles, in the right direction.

We also heard constantly of hell. Before football games, we recited the Lord's Prayer, complete with the part about deliver-·

ing us from evil. Afterward we knelt and prayed there on the field and half the town—the parents and teachers and preachers—knelt as well, heads bowed, eyes closed. Every civic ceremony, from the Christmas parade to the country's bicentennial, opened with a short prayer, in Jesus's name.

In Sunday school Mrs. Dupont told us of the dangers of rock music and *Dungeons & Dragons*. Apparently power chords and rolling dice were gateways to Satan, or maybe witchcraft. I'd like to dismiss Mrs. Dupont as a crackpot, but outside of the Sunday school classroom, she spoke of God's great love for us all, and it occurs to me now that she could be both crackpot and caring—the two don't preclude one another.

In history class we learned how Columbus brought Christianity to the heathens in the New World, none of our books ever mentioning how many Indigenous peoples were killed, either through murder or disease, the unspoken argument being that since they were savages they didn't matter. Mrs. Born-Again said our nation had been founded on Christian principles, forgetting (or never bothering to learn) that many of the Founding Fathers were deists who viewed Christ more like a clock than any sort of savior.

One summer afternoon walking home from the swimming pool, Tommy Halford and I were stopped by a man who wanted to tell us about hell. The summer heat had sucked all the joy out of life, and here was a man in a suit to tell us there were places even hotter. His hair was plastered to his head, and he carried a little pamphlet with an image on it I still remember: three stick figures, all different colors. One was white to represent the purity of Christ. The next was red to represent our sinful natures.

The last one was on fire. It was a simple drawing but somehow conveyed the torture of hell, and Tommy and I tried to laugh but went silent on the walk home. That night we said we would take church more seriously because we didn't want to burn, and I remember how late we stayed up, wondering if there were really a way to keep from it.

It seemed there wasn't. Every story said the end was inevitable. Either we would burn in the lake of fire or fire would fall from the sky. Everyone I knew was afraid: of fire, of war and death and disease and annihilation. Because our preachers pronounced it over and over. Because it was on the nightly news. Because Reagan said the Soviet Union was evil, a phrase he must have heard from the religious right and the Moral Majority and the Christian Coalition, who believed that the state should be guided by the church.

To achieve this end, they taught us we weren't worthy of living without the love of Jesus to guide us, and these teachings, from the top, came trickling down to us in a way Reagan's tax cuts never did.

So we believed them. Every morning prayer at school said so. Every kneeling after every football game reinforced the idea that only through Christ could we be saved. We lived in a town where grown men accosted little boys on the street to tell them how long they would burn. Reagan ended his 1980 Republican nomination acceptance speech with a silent prayer, followed by the words "God Bless America," ushering in the age of American patriotism predicated on the belief that we have His blessing. Reagan courted conservative Christians away from Jimmy Carter and won the popular vote on a religious wave, which meant that all the leaders of our country, from public school teacher to president, believed in the inherent righteousness of the United States.

With righteousness comes right, and with right comes might. Our missiles were aimed at the skies, and we believed, with all the faith of followers, that if the fire ever fell, it was by design. God had planned our end, so if the atheist Soviets across the ever-narrowing sea wanted fire, then by God they could have it.

In ninth grade, reading Dante, I came upon the final circle of hell, where Satan is encased in ice. I was fourteen. It was 1986, and though the political climate in the Soviet Union was warming, here we hung onto our long-held beliefs. In the accompanying Gustave Doré image of Satan encased in ice, Satan looks more bored than burning, more amused than in agony, which led me to believe that ice had to be better than fire—surely in a nuclear winter we could find enough fire to stay warm.

Seeing it also made me wonder if we could rewrite what we always believed. As I had grown older, I had begun to question the contradictions: why we believed that we fought for peace, how destroying the world would save it. So I wondered if hell could be made of ice, or at least different levels of it like in Dante, since murderers surely had to be punished more severely than masturbators. I wondered if the Bible had it wrong and hell was just a dark hole or a slightly unpleasant place. I'd read enough mythology by then to discover different kinds of hell, and I began to wonder if the Bible, like Dante's Inferno, wasn't fiction, stories to steer our lives toward goodness, not station us in a land of hatred.

Somehow we had gotten off track, I thought. If God was loving, He had no reason to destroy us. It seemed ridiculous to say in one breath that God was a vengeful God, and in another that Jesus loved the little children, "red and yellow, black and white."

But some of us—young boys, for example—after being told so many times we're unworthy, begin to believe it. After so long

hearing you're sinful, it's easy to turn to sin. After so long hearing the world will be destroyed, maybe you want to destroy it.
And after so long hearing there's another world, you can stop
caring about this one.

That summer an older cousin sent me a shirt his fraternity
had made. On the shirt, an eagle had a bear in its talons, and
above the picture were the words "Ruck the Fussians." I loved
that shirt. When it came in the mail, I wore it everywhere my
parents would let me; it made me unafraid. I had begun to consider joining the military. If the Fussians made me afraid, I would
ruck them. I couldn't rid myself of the fear of fire, so I would
embrace it instead. I would wrap hatred around me because I
felt small and afraid, and I was tired of feeling small and afraid.

Three years later I joined the Arkansas Army National Guard.
I was in basic training when Saddam Hussein invaded Kuwait in
August of 1990. That morning our drill sergeants called us all
together. We'd spent six weeks shooting at cutouts of Soviet soldiers, stabbing them with our bayonets, tossing hand grenades
at them. Now a new war loomed on the horizon, so we swung
our old hatreds toward a different corner of the world.

In the buildup to the Gulf War, we forgot about the Soviets.
Now we worried about the Iraqi Republican Guard. SCUD missiles falling on Tel Aviv. Biological and chemical weapons, and
it occurred to me later how easily the shift occurred. That we
always need someone to call evil so we can call ourselves good.

Ten years after the Gulf War ended, two airplanes would
fly into the Twin Towers, and our country would clamor for
retaliation. George W. Bush would claim Iraq and Afghanistan
and North Korea were evil empires, and we would invade two
of the three. We've been rattling our sabers in those countries
ever since. I fear now we'll be rattling them forever. That we'll
believe or do anything if it makes us feel safer.

In the '8os we were told everything we knew and loved would die. That the Soviets were evil. That listening to rock music was a sin but bombing other countries was sanctioned.

No wonder then we wanted the world to burn. We were small and afraid and told the world was destined to burn anyway. That God demanded it. There was no reason to stand against what was coming, no reason to do anything other than consume, since everything would be consumed anyway. There was no reason to save a world that was doomed, especially when the next one waited for us. It never occurred to us we might use up the next one too, that perhaps the waiting doom came not from biblical prophecy but our own profligacy. That our sense of entitlement made us the evil ones. That whatever war or afterworld waited for us was of our own making.

# New Words for the New World

When your sleeves bunch up while putting on your coat, it's called a scrauntlet, or malsleevance. Gripping the shirt sleeve to keep it from bunching is called cuffling.

Saying the same word at the same time as somebody else is a jinxing; trying to get past someone at the elevator door is a juggling, a side-step, a beshuffling.

Not getting enough likes on social media is being screenied, and when a less important post than yours gets more shares it's an inter-rage.

Your daughter's first steps are a jottering and her first tooth is a trying and the way her fine hair disappears when it gets wet is a willowing. Perffluvium is a new baby's smell. Morlorn, the feeling on the first day of November when the last leaves rattle toward the forest floor. Azura is the color of the sky when it's so blue it hurts to look at it, on days you feel you could float away on the wind.

The fear you felt as a child is a dissuffering, a phobling, a forefright. Growing up in the uncertain world of the '70s was severitude, not to be confused with the servitude we all thought the Soviets would shackle us in. Missiles falling was a frightening, and the end of the world was a finality, not unlike the forever we first heard about in Sunday service, which we called borrific. Surviving those times to carry all your unwanted anxieties into adulthood is encumbrishment; still remembering where they came from is a conjuring.

Parcheron was the feel of your grandmother's ancient papery skin, and blemings were the bruises she wore around the IV needles. Emphysematic was how she sounded in her last days, and dreaden was the feeling you got when her breath caught in her throat—airfloat was how you felt every time she drew another.

Corrified is when you hear the screech of tires as your children are playing in the front yard or any time there's an amber alert, breaking news, a school shot up, which is a shredding, of heart and hope.

When you fall out of love after twenty years, it's a dawning, or a leavening, depending on what you decide to do. If you end up staying together because it's too hard to move on, that's a shielding, and the weeks you slept on the couch while wondering is called a caesura.

When the kids never call from college, that's a sylon, and when the phone rings late at night, that's a voidwind. When you drink too much remembering how small they seemed on the first day of school, that's maundering, and the day they were born is a gripping in the same way their tiny hands held your smallest finger.

We need a word for loneliness that doesn't rely on the word alone. That doesn't sound like love. Say it's azura. Or morlorn. Loss isn't the keys you can't find but the hook where hers used to hang. There's a reason the heart is the symbol for love, a reason we say it's somewhere near the lungs.

Nulling is the terrible news we hear every day and shaddering the silence that won't let us sleep. Intercurses are the words we say when the horribleness won't end and begrief the feeling after the intercurses, when the sylon sets in and the voidwind comes down.

We're always searching for the right language, the right words. I don't know if we need more words or a better understanding of our insides. I don't know what new world we've wandered into. Only that sometimes I feel hapshaken. Or contumbled. I don't know which way the sky lies. I don't have the words I need, so I make them up: dolorment and bewhining and love-drunk. Hope-filled, heart-hurt, joybilant. We're always inventing new words, always brushing up against places we never thought we'd be, whether it's our own mortality or all the slings and arrows of outrageous fortune.

We don't need a word for those. That's just breathing. It's walking around in our thin skins, our hearts holding at the point blood begins, at the place in the body we store all the emotions we can't explain.

# Breakdown

In the early '80s, about the time I started seventh grade, an odd thing happened in my small, white, Southern town: from its inception on the streets of South Bronx, breakdancing filtered down to us, and suddenly we were spinning and popping, carrying cardboard boxes so the concrete didn't tear up our clothes. This was a style of dancing we'd never imagined existed. We had heard rap music from Run-D.M.C., and even Blondie had gotten into the business with "Rapture," the first rap song ever to hit number 1 on the Billboard 100, but we'd never seen breakdancing, or the clothes that came with it—the bandanas and headbands, the wrist scarves and baggy pants.

This was a town with gun racks in the windows of pickup trucks, where high school students were allowed a skip day when deer season started. Our parents listened to country music and drove thirty miles to get loaded because liquor wasn't allowed in our Christian town, and I'll say now we looked upon anything outside our cultural purview of camouflage and Coors Light as both highly sophisticated and highly dangerous, a thing to both admire and fear. Because of this, we didn't eat wheat bread or drink dark beer. Men entering middle-age were still mad about Woodstock and hippies and marijuana cigarettes. Breakdancing then, and rap music and hats worn sideways on the head, were suspect here at the same time they were fashionable there, since it all originated outside the walls of our village.

In that summer before my seventh-grade year, we were all trying desperately hard to be cool. The Cold War was still frigid, but none of us were. We had all broken out at the same time, but our breakouts were of acne instead of our inner selves. No one could decide who he wanted to be—we all only wanted to be like everyone else. My voice couldn't decide what it wanted to be either, whether the low tones of a man or the high pitch of a kid. I wanted a mustache but could only find fine fuzz on my upper lip, the kind the older men said a cat could lick off. In the cafes on Saturday morning, they drank coffee and decried the declining world.

This was the summer I had joined the swim team, not realizing it would involve swimming. I thought we would just hang out at the pool, growing darker and occasionally flinging wet hair from our eyes. In my first race ever, I dove in and my swim trunks, newly purchased by my caring mother because she wanted me to look sleek as I cut through the water, came down to my ankles. My ass flashed like an albino seal, and for the first fifty meters I went along one-armed, trying to hoist my britches up with the other.

It was my last race. I managed to get my shorts up before I was arrested for indecent exposure, but my swim hopes had been dashed. Retreating from the laughter, I left the pool and walked outside into the awful heat and loneliness.

On the basketball court next to the swimming pool, a crowd had gathered. I thought first there was a fight coming. There was always a fight coming in my hometown. All through elementary we had watched fights after school behind the library, and all through senior high we would watch them at the park, long lines of cars coming down the hill from the high school, even the girls who were going to good colleges, even the guys considering seminary.

There were perhaps a dozen kids in the circle. They had a loud boom box, and it was playing a song I would come to recognize as "Jam on It" by a band named Newcleus. Perhaps *band* isn't the right word, but we didn't know the right words then. Despite Deborah Harry's appropriation, we didn't know anything about the culture, the lyrics, or the rhythms of rap music. We didn't know how breakin' was born, or how it came here, to small-town Arkansas, where, well, we were all white. Super white. In high school, a Norwegian exchange student would live in town for a year, but he was whiter than we were, though more knowledgeable of the world due to having flown so far to get to our town.

By the end of the year—this was 1984—Hollywood would jump on the break-wagon and bring us *Breakin', Beat Street,* and *Body Rock,* but until then, what was happening here was a total mystery. The kids with the boom box were from Fort Smith, the closest thing to a city we had, about an hour away. They had come down for the swim meet, but, like me, had wandered away from the water.

In the center of the circle, a kid my age was dying. Or so I thought at first. I would later learn he was doing the dolphin, but then it looked as if—because I had never seen anything like it—he was flopping on the beach. He was still wet from his first race, so I'll forgive myself the misunderstanding. From a full stand he fell forward, curving his body to take the impact of hitting the ground, knees first, then down to his stomach, his shoulders, and finally rising again like a rocker arm, body curving back up to almost full height, then down again, the hot asphalt hardly hurting him. I thought it a magic trick. I wanted to see more.

The next breaker spun on his head, and the one after that seemed to float on his feet. I'd later learn these were amateurs compared to Ozone and Turbo from *Breakin'* and *Breakin' 2: Electric Boogaloo,* or any number of breakers who'd helped develop the style, but they seemed to move on a different plane. Their joints popped when they moved, and their feet were fluid, like watching water run. They played "Jam on It" again and again, and "Rapper's Delight" by the Sugarhill Gang, and the circle grew bigger as more and more kids came in to watch.

By the end of the swim meet, when the tall pimply kid who owned the radio turned it off and the crowd dispersed and our parents came to pick us up, I was trying to remember the lyrics to "Rapper's Delight." My mother asked what I was doing with my arms. Looking in the rearview mirror, she must have thought I was either convulsing or had swallowed so much water I was becoming liquid. I had learned the names of some of the moves, and when I told her I was doing the wave, she didn't ask what it was, or what it meant or where it had come from, but I could see her worrying that there was something seriously wrong with me.

By the time school started a few weeks later, the first bandannas and wristbands had appeared. One group of girls wore Michael Jackson gloves and tried to moonwalk in the courtyard, and by late September the first breakdance circles appeared like crop formations, signaling there might be aliens among us.

There were only a few dancers. I don't mean to make it sound like we were all poppin' and lockin', but we all watched. The circle would grow bigger and bigger as Joe Foster attempted, for the hundredth time, a headspin, which usually ended with someone being kicked in the face as he flailed about, or as

Stacy Gaston performed his mime dance, in which he not only pretended to be locked inside an invisible box but also, since he had nothing else to do in there, pretended to masturbate, complete with climax in the form of spit.

In the hallways, Melanie Hart moonwalked to class. Madison Stenn did that Michael Jackson toe stand, and Amy Bishop wore the jacket from the "Thriller" video. On the bus to basketball games, we listened to Run-D.M.C.

One Saturday at Walmart, two break dancers gave an exhibition, and I remember thinking there was no turning back now. Even at twelve, I knew Walmart was the last bastion of conservatism, and here pop culture—Black pop culture—had infiltrated it, even though the break dancers were white. They wore slick vinyl track suits with bandannas tied around their wrists and ankles, and the women watching gasped when they did the worm and the windmill but wandered away when they began to explain how the movement started.

By 1985 even Mr. Rogers was breakin' (seriously, look it up). Run-D.M.C. released *King of Rock*, which hit number 52 on the Billboard charts, and number 12 on the top R&B/Hip-Hop. LL Cool J released his debut album, *Radio*, long before he started solving crimes on NCIS. Schoolly-D came out with "P.S.K. (What Does It Mean)?" one of the first gangsta rap songs.

While our parents were listening to George Strait and Hank Williams Jr., we were experimenting with early Ice-T and bootlegged Beastie Boys. That summer my best friend and I stayed up late watching *The Breakfast Club* and *Better Off Dead*, the whitest movies we knew, but we secretly loved *The Last Dragon*, in which a Black kid named Bruce Leroy is forced to fight the Harlem Shogun Sho'Nuff.

At the homecoming dance, Stacy Gaston performed his locked-in-a-box masturbation. Joe Foster had almost mastered the headspin and was working on the windmill. Melanie and Madison moonwalked even to the slow songs. The DJ kept playing "Beat Street Breakdown" between "Billy Jean" and "Purple Rain," and each time the circle formed someone would enter, imitating what they'd seen filtering down from a world they would never know.

A few years later gangster rap, in the form of N.W.A., had reached us, and we walked the halls singing "Fuck tha Police" and "Dope Man" without understanding the anger coming out of Compton. (When I saw *Boyz n the Hood,* I wanted the shirt Cuba Gooding wears that says "Crenshaw," not knowing it was the name of the street that cuts through South Central.) We listened to Motown through the '70s but knew nothing of Detroit and the exodus from the South that had helped start that sound; how Black people fleeing the segregation we still lived in settled in northern cities, creating Motown, Harlem jazz, and now rap coming from Queens and breakin' from South Bronx.

Perhaps I sensed even then that in white America we were choosing to accept only what we thought were the cool parts of Black culture, co-opting them as our own. There's a reason Blondie hit number 1 on the Billboard charts long before any Black rappers, the same reason Vanilla Ice—a name that managed to proclaim whiteness twice in two words—was the next to do it, followed by Marky Mark—who twice proclaimed himself "Mark." "Rapture" wasn't a rap song—it was a pop song with a rap part, a sample to see how it would be received. It would take ten years for rap music to make it anywhere close to mainstream.

But none of that really mattered to us. We were caught up in the culture coming at us from Compton. Maybe because it was an alternative to the culture of war that was all around us. Living near that army base with live-fire exercises every summer, our fathers cursing the communists who wanted to destroy us. Every politician looked exactly like our white fathers, so it's no wonder we were all confused, that we wanted to get away from our whiteness and war as much as we wanted to be cool, cool meaning, in this case, not consumed by nuclear fire.

Whatever the reason, we called each other homeboy and crackhead. Girls were strawberries, or fly. Shit was dope or wack, depending. We dissed anyone who wasn't chill. We stole the language because we could, because we wanted it, because we wanted what we considered the coolness of Black culture without actually being Black, because we knew, even isolated as we were in our small white town, that to be Black was to be in danger, to be targeted by police and dismissed by people like us, and that the only way to get anyone to hear you was to express your life in music or art because no one was listening any other way.

Where we were, we had it all. When we weren't listening to Run-D.M.C., we had the other '80s we could switch to, A-ha and Wham and Bananarama and A Flock of Seagulls with their flopped-over hair, as if the '70s had synthesized into something else. I still don't know what it was, but we loved it too, even the country music our parents forced us to listen to on the way to school in the morning. We had the hair bands and rock ballads, the keyboards and clapping of John Cougar Mellencamp, a name that's too depressing now to try to explicate. It was as if we didn't have a culture of our own and so adopted pieces from everywhere, trying to make ourselves into something else because we didn't like who we seemed destined to become.

Six weeks before the '85 Superbowl, the Chicago Bears recorded their own rap song, "The Super Bowl Shuffle." This was right about the time my high school football team made it all the way to the state championship game, where we would go up against Marvell, a mostly Black high school from the eastern part of the state. The Bears' rap was not as good as their football, but for some reason we all accepted it—I heard it more times than I care to count, and though it's shudderingly bad, I remember how much we loved it. Sweetness came first, followed by Willie Gault, who was followed by Singletary, and in the background the other Bears kept up that white-guy slide shuffle throughout the video.

It's so, so bad. The lyrics are even worse, as is the fake instrument playing, but no one seemed to notice. Caught up in the wave of other bad '80s music, we didn't realize that the producers were just trying to cash in on the "sudden" emergence of rap. I'm surprised Singletary didn't do the dolphin across the stage.

In February of '86, "The Super Bowl Shuffle" hit number 41 on the Billboard 100, and it spawned a wave of imitators, from the '86 Houston Rockets and their "Rocket Strut" to the "Seminole Rap" of Florida State in '88. Everyone, it seemed, wanted to rap. By the end of the '80s, whole groups of white people were rapping in commercials, proving that we'll do anything if we think it'll make us look cool (it didn't).

A few days after "The Super Bowl Shuffle" was recorded, we went to the state championship game, a whole caravan of cars listening mostly to country music while our parents smoked in the front seats. In the stadium we segregated ourselves by color: I mean my team was purple and gold and Marvell was blue and white, but I also mean we sat white on one side of the stadium, and they sat Black on the other. The respective cheerleaders were introducing themselves to one another, and the players were shaking hands on the field, but we sat staring, waiting for the game to begin so we could pretend it was every day we interacted with Black people.

I don't remember much of the game, only that the other team was bigger and faster than we were, and every time they scored we got a little madder, retreating into our old insecurities a little further. When the Marvell band took the field at halftime, we were down two touchdowns and seething, so it didn't surprise me when, as their drum line began to dance, the old men from my town stood staring open-mouthed, as if they didn't quite know what was happening.

It didn't last long. Maybe someone did a backflip. Maybe someone did the dolphin. Whatever happened, I realized our parents didn't know what we'd been doing—the music we were listening to, the culture we were captivated by. Maybe it's not fair to say they didn't know anything existed outside our postage stamp of land, but it is fair to say they didn't give it much thought, sure as they were that we would follow in their non-moonwalking footsteps.

At the end of the game, we filed out of the stands, our egos bruised and beer-battered. In the bathroom a long line of men who'd been sipping smuggled whisky were emptying themselves into troughs along the wall, and I waited in line, a small kid who still looked up to the men around him, even as he began to understand their ignorance might end the world.

"Did you see that shit at halftime?" one man said, shaking his head. His face, lined by wind and weather and declining middle age, was so close to the wall over the urinal he had his hat turned backward, which made me wonder how far he could see in front of him. "I mean, did you see them shucking and jiving?"

Of course he said more. There were slurs. I'm not afraid of telling you what they were. I'm just choosing to remember it differently, in the hope that my changing the story might change the men I looked up to as a boy, force them to see the world through a different-colored lens. I'd wish to remember that he finished and flushed and went to wash his hands, where he looked at himself in the mirror. That he went out into the passageways of the big stadium and saw his kids waiting for him, and then, to cheer them up, moonwalked all the way to his car.

# Dead Baby

## 1. Jokes

How do you make a dead baby float?

Two scoops of ice cream, one scoop of dead baby.

He didn't float. I know that, even if I never knew what he looked like, lying there in the closed casket. I have always assumed it was the funeral director—whoever does the embalming, the floating of fluids through the small veins of the infant body—who decided my grandmother could not stand to see the choke marks around his neck, or the bruises that damaged his brain.

How many babies does it take to paint a house?

Depends how hard you throw them.

He wasn't thrown. He was shaken, then punched. In the courtroom the medical examiner outlined the four bruises, spaced like knuckles, on his forehead. If you were standing out in the hallway of the old court building, the crying from inside might have sounded like laughter.

How did the dead baby cross the road?

He was stapled to the chicken.

Perhaps he tried to cross the road. He was only eighteen months old, but perhaps he tried. It's possible the abuse that would lead to his death had already begun or that children instinctually know the dark hearts of those who would hurt them, which makes me wonder what the boy thought of those who did not help. For many years I would blame myself for not knowing. I wasn't much more than a child myself, but some nights, near the new light of morning, I wonder why we never knew the boy was being abused. When he was handed to his stepfather, he would begin to cry. He would hold his arms out for the person handing him over to take him back, so I say it's possible he was trying to cross the road. To get to the other side.

If a tree falls on a dead baby in the forest and no one is around to hear it, is it still hilarious?

In the courtroom, the stepfather said he found the door unlatched. He turned around only for a second, and when he went outside the boy lay under a pile of wood.

"It looked like he tried to climb the woodpile and it fell on him," the stepfather said.

"How did the knuckle bruises get on his forehead?" the prosecutor asked.

What present do you buy for a dead baby?

A dead puppy.

He would only ever have one birthday. The cake, the candle, the wrapping paper strewn around the room while the family looks on. One, and no more. He would be dead before his second birthday, although we can count Christmas, I suppose. Imagine a Christmas morning, snow on the ground. The quiet waking in a house hung not with stockings but with some darkness already alive in the hallways and living rooms. It snowed on the day he died too. So maybe that's not the best image. Instead, I think of the puppy he may have gotten at some point. I try not to think how he never made it to that birthday. Or any of the others.

What's pink and red and taps on the window?
    A baby in a microwave.

A woman near Dallas left her children in a locked car in the Texas heat while she went grocery shopping. She claimed she was only gone for a few minutes. When she came back, her children were dead. In her defense she said she did not know they would die. I would like to heap scorn and condemnation on this woman, but we left the child with the stepfather. Because we did not know what would happen, could never have foreseen the violence built upon the boy's body.

## 2. History, Part 1: Killers

In 1999, ten years after the boy was killed, Colombian serial killer Luis Garavito admitted to the murder of 147 young boys. He approached them on the streets and lured them into the country, where he bound their hands, tortured, raped, and murdered them, often by decapitation. In his courtroom testimony, he said he had been physically and emotionally abused by his father. Garavito's girlfriend claimed he got along well with her child. He was sentenced to 1,853 years in prison.

## Mrs. Dyer, The Baby Farmer

The old baby farmer has been executed,
It's quite time that she was put out of the way,
She was a bad woman, it is not disputed,
Not a word in her favour can anyone say.

That old baby farmer the wretch Mrs. Dyer,
At the Old Bailey her wages is paid,
In times long ago we'd have made a big fire,
And roasted so nicely that wicked old jade.

British serial killer Amelia Dyer murdered as many as four hundred babies between 1869 and 1896. Trained as a nurse, she turned to "baby farming" when her husband passed away, taking in single mothers and babies for a fee. After an arrest for negligence and a six months' hard labor sentence, she began to adopt unwanted babies and murder them. She wrapped tape around their necks and then threw them in the Thames or buried them in her backyard. Sometimes she drugged them so they would remain silent until suffocated. The 1834 Poor Law Amendment Act had taken away any financial obligations to fathers, and poor women had little recourse when finding themselves pregnant. They went to women like Amelia Dyer, or they "made angels" of their babies by suffocating them and claiming they were stillborn, since Victorian doctors could not diagnose the difference.

## 3. Etymology

O'er the rugged mountain's brow,
Clara threw the twins she nursed,
and remarked "I wonder now,
which will reach the bottom first."

—Harry Graham, *Ruthless Rhymes
for Heartless Homes*, 1899

In his essay "The Dead Baby Joke Cycle," folklorist Alan Dundes traces the history of the dead baby joke. He theorizes the rise of sick humor in America—of which he claims there is a long-standing tradition—is a reaction to the failure of Americans to discuss disease and death openly. Dundes writes, "It would seem obvious enough that the higher the incidence of euphemism, the greater the anxiety about the subject matter." Put simply, we laugh about what we can't talk about because the pain is too great.

Although Dundes cannot pinpoint the beginnings of sick humor, he points to the "Little Willie" quatrains as one of the earliest examples. In 1899 English poet Harry Graham published *Ruthless Rhymes for Heartless Homes,* which may have inspired the "Little Wille" quatrain, and which included several verses referring to infanticide:

Willie split the baby's head,
to see if brains were gray or red,
Mother, troubled, said to father,
"Children are an awful bother."

Willie, with a thirst for gore,
nailed the baby to the door.

Mother said, with humor quaint,
"Willie, dear, don't spoil the paint."

The "Little Willie" verses, Dundes writes, lasted well into the 1930s. More cruel joke collections came in the '50s and '60s. In the 1970s the sick joke manifested itself in many forms, including sick Jesus jokes, sick Southerner jokes (often racist in nature), and sick doctor jokes, in which the punchline informs the patient of some terrible mistake the doctor has made.

Here I would also add the fear we all felt from nuclear war. At school we told "stupid Russian" jokes: about the Soviet parachutist who deploys his chute too late; about Soviet missiles that explode on the runway, thus never finding US soil; about the Soviet astronauts no smarter than the first dog to orbit the Earth. What we were trying to do was find a way to live with the fear. And since we could not understand how men could send missiles that might burn every baby alive, we laughed.

Dundes outlines a history of sick jokes but does not attempt to answer—most likely because there is no definite answer—when and where the dead baby joke, in its modern form, arose. What he does provide is analysis. Many of the dead baby jokes have to do with getting rid of babies: placing them in garbage bags or down disposals. Many also contain references to babies being ground up by machines, which might point to a fear of modern technology.

Dundes also makes the case—since the popularity of dead baby jokes rose in the '70s—that the jokes refer to legalized abortion and the increased availability of birth control. Legalized abortion, along with publicized contraception and sex education classes, made teenagers more aware of the dangers of pregnancy. Women's liberation ideology, by insisting that motherhood was not the only available career path for women, might also have played a role.

The price of all this, Dundes says, may have been dead baby jokes, told to assuage the guilt over preventing the creation of life. Modern technology—abortion procedures, contraception—allowed women to dispose of children. Razors might represent home abortions, plastic bags being trapped in a condom or diaphragm.

Folklore, Dundes writes, "is a reflection of the age in which it flourishes. . . . If anything is sick, it is the society which produces sick humor. . . . Our concern therefore should not be with dead baby jokes but with dead babies."

Dundes's article was published in 1979, ten years before the boy was found dead beneath the woodpile. In another article, this one from 1988, barely a year before the boy was killed, Dundes says, "What scares us, we seek to make ridiculous. What's ridiculous can't hurt us."

Which is, of course, ridiculous.

## 4. History, Part 2

The nurses at the emergency room called the police, and the police took the stepfather into custody. Two of the nurses would later testify. They would explain that the bruises on the body were consistent with child abuse, and this makes me wonder what awful things the nurses had seen, what jokes they told each other to get through the night.

My family tends to laugh at funerals. The weeping and wiping of eyes has always manifested itself in humor. We do not find funerals funny, but always there's a moment in which we forget the solemnity of the occasion. My uncle tells a joke. My mother tells him to hush, but then they are both laughing. If you didn't know better, you would say they were crying, but because we are private people, the crying comes later, when we are alone. Which is where the crying always comes from, I say—being alone, which makes me wonder what fear the boy felt when he was left alone with the stepfather.

We did not laugh at his funeral. But afterward, we stood outside and talked of violence.

I've spent much of my life trying to find the world funny. The rest of the time I am trying to make sense of it. This may seem a contradiction in light of what I've outlined here, but let me tell you: it's the only thing that allows me to continue, although sometimes I wonder if we continue only because the alternative is too awful to consider.

## 5. Beginnings and Endings

Yo mama so ugly, she had to get the baby drunk so that she could breastfeed it.

Another series of jokes that struck us as funny during these years were "Yo Mama" jokes. If I were to analyze these jokes alongside the others, I'd have to say something about beginnings and endings, birth and giving birth, life and death. As if we are always wondering what would happen if we weren't alive. As if we were constantly in fear of being erased, which may be why, in our formative years, when we were trying to find our place in the world, we laughed so often at death, and at those who gave us life.

Yo mama so old, she walked into an antique store and they kept her.

When the boy died, he knew fewer than a dozen words. *Mama* was one of them, as was *hurt*. *Father* was not in his vocabulary.

Yo mama so ugly she turned Medusa into stone.

But beauty is in the eye of the beholder, so I imagine how the boy must have looked at his mother. I imagine how her heart turned to stone when she saw her son on the hospital table with tubes snaked down his throat.

Yo mama so ugly when she took a bath the water jumped out.

And yet I imagine bath time for the boy: the squeaky toys, the wet hair, the mother sitting on the edge of the tub. This before the beating, the frantic trip to the emergency room where the nurses noticed the nature of the bruises. I imagine the mother singing in a soft voice. In those early days, the boy knew no other world than his mother, which may be why all children know what *mother* means, even if they can't say it.

Let me say I no longer know what to find funny.

Let me say that none of this is funny now. That there's a hole where the boy used to be. That we all have holes drilled into us, and we never know when another one will appear. But the day before the phone call came, I was walking down the hall of high school while my best friend told me how you got a dead baby into a bucket and how you got it out, how many dead babies it took to change a lightbulb, what you call a dead baby pinned to the wall, what the difference is between a dead baby and a pizza, a dead baby and a bagel, a bucket of gravel and a bucket of dead babies, on and on and on until there seemed no end to the amount of human cruelty in the world. Or maybe we knew even then that we laugh at what we fear the most. And we did laugh. We threw our heads back and screamed. We slapped each other on the back. We told everyone around us about the dead babies, and they told everyone else, until it seemed we were all laughing. We had not yet seen the horrors coming for us or how we'd handle them. We had not yet wondered if we would be able to go on. So we laughed, the same way we laughed at the world we were yet to understand, although maybe we did foresee something of the future, because the way I remember it, we laughed so hard we cried.

# Cold Cola Wars

Kevin Sloak liked Pepsi, so I didn't like Kevin Sloak. Heather Davis liked Pepsi too, and despite the fact that she had developed a crush on me, I couldn't bring myself to like a girl who drank Pepsi, because Pepsi was sold in the Soviet Union, which made Heather a traitor to everything we held dear in the summer of 1986, and it made Kevin-shitting-Sloak a communist.

We didn't know then about the Kitchen Debate between Nixon and Khrushchev, or anything about unfettered capitalism. We didn't know Pepsi had, in the early '60s, claimed to be of our parents' generation, that it was one of the first companies to aim its marketing campaigns at lifestyles, and the lifestyle it aimed at in the '80s was us, the next generation. What we did know was that Coke wanted to teach the world to sing and that Pepsi had nearly killed Michael Jackson in 1984. We knew that instead of the cool Coke candle commercial, Pepsi constantly aired those stupid taste tests on TV.

But what earned our unfettered ire was that besides being sold in the Soviet Union, Pepsi was the Soviets' preferred drink. Even without the King of Pop disaster and the mind-numbing commercials appearing every eight minutes, the fact that communists drank it was reason to hate it. We'd been taught all through elementary school to fear everything Soviet, including, but not limited to, colas, and since Pepsi had manufacturing plants in Moscow and had signed an exclusive deal to distribute their soda to the Soviets and ship Soviet vodka here, we reasoned, as red-blooded Americans, it was our patriotic duty to not only boycott Pepsi but to harass Kevin Sloak at lunchtime, where he sat on the front steps of the school with his sad papersack lunch.

"Pepsi even sounds Soviet," I might have said, late summer of '86, to Kevin Sloak, with a few of my bigger friends looking on. "And so does Sloak." But Kevin was one of those kids who wore a trench coat and fingerless gloves to school in August, and so kept his head down until we wandered off looking for easier fare, someone we could make cry because, it seems to me now, that was what we did in eighth grade in 1986. The world was always at war and so were we. Pepsi fought with Coke and the US fought with the USSR and we all fought with each other because we couldn't fight ourselves. Our bodies had morphed us into monsters and our faces had broken out from all the sodas we consumed and we hated everything about the time, even our own insides.

So we wandered off to another part of the steps, waiting for the bell to ring, where I would go to class and sit by Jennifer S., who drank Dr. Pepper, which was bottled by Pepsi in some places and Coke in others, and therefore a gray area. There was no internet then, so we didn't know the whole history of the Cola Wars and the Cold War and how our own needs drove them both, nor did we know the name Pepsi-Cola was an amalgamation of "dyspepsia" and "kola nuts," but I'm sure we could have come up with something clever, like "stomach nuts," had we known.

It began like this: On July 24, 1959, Soviet First Secretary Nikita

Khrushchev drank a Pepsi. In a cultural exchange program designed to promote understanding between the two countries, the USSR held an exhibition in New York. The United States held their own in Moscow, featuring American products: cars, art, fashion, and a model American house. A number of companies sponsored exhibits and booths, including IBM and Pepsi.

In the kitchen of the model house, then Vice President Richard Nixon and Khrushchev discussed the differences in their countries. At one point, Nixon led Khrushchev to a display of Pepsi, one mixed with "American" water, the other with "Russian." Khrushchev continually denigrated capitalism, but, as the story goes, he loved Pepsi.

And, as capitalism and politics so often collude, the idea to get Khrushchev to drink Pepsi came from an advertising executive named Donald Kendall, who saw the Soviet Union as a vast new territory for Pepsi to conquer. It took Kendall over a decade to do it, but in 1972 he negotiated a deal to send Pepsi to the Soviet Union, where it would be bottled locally. He also locked out Coca-Cola, Pepsi's biggest rival, until 1985. Pepsi became the first capitalist product available in the Soviet Union, but because the Russian ruble was worthless in Western markets and Soviet capital could not be used abroad, the United States got Stolichnaya vodka as a trade.

By the mid-'80s, about the time I stomp angrily into the picture, antagonizing Kevin Sloak on the front steps of the high school, Soviets were drinking Pepsi as often as my friends and I stole our parents' Stoli vodka. I suppose it didn't occur to us what hypocrites we were to criticize Kevin for his Pepsi at the same time we skipped school to get soused on Stoli, but I'll say here that with alcohol at that age, you take what you can get, and let the finer points of boycotting fall to the side, much like you will later, probably in a ditch somewhere.

I digress.

The problem with the Pepsi deal, besides our small-town paranoia of anything Soviet-made that didn't contain alcohol, was that the Soviet Union couldn't pay. The trading of vodka worked until more Americans began boycotting Soviet products over the Soviet invasion of Afghanistan, hurting Pepsi's profit on Stoli distribution, which meant that the Soviets needed to find a new means of exchange.

What they came up with were ships. In the spring of 1989, only a few months before I would join the military, the Soviet Union gave Pepsi seventeen old submarines and three warships to keep their deal going. Pepsi eventually sold the warships. But for a brief moment, like the fifteen minutes of fame we're all supposed to get, Pepsi had the sixth-largest navy in the world. Kevin Sloak still wore a trench coat to school and possibly carried a switchblade. With the acne attacking him and the anger he wore around, we were afraid he might retaliate if we poked fun at his Pepsi. Michael Jackson had recovered fully and was now making commercials in Russia. Which meant that, despite the Berlin Wall coming down, it seemed as if the Soviet Union had won a different kind of war.

If Pepsi represented the Soviet Union, then Coca-Cola represented America. By the time I was born, the famous Coke commercial about teaching the world to sing was already a year old, but in the mid-'70s a new version aired around the holidays for several years. A third version featuring the original singers and their children appeared during the 1990 Superbowl, a few weeks before I turned eighteen, meaning that song, like me, somehow survived the '80s.

It also marked it. After every Little League game, we lined up outside the concession stand for a Coke. We might have ordered Sprite or Sundrop or a "suicide," but it came in a red paper cup with Coca-Cola written on it. Movie theaters in the mid-'80s used these same cups, meaning we watched *Wargames* and *The Manhattan Project* and *The Terminator*—all movies about the end of the world—while drinking Coke. They were served at high school basketball games I secretly hoped Jennifer S. would show up to so I could buy her a Dr. Pepper, and at football games where Kevin Sloak leaned alone against the chain-link fence behind the bleachers.

Our mothers gave us Sprite when we were sick, along with chicken noodle soup, which I still want when I'm sick and lying on the couch, home from work at 10 a.m. watching *The Price Is Right*. When they weren't tending to us, our mothers drank Tab, a diet drink, so they could watch their weight. Our stepfathers mixed Evan Williams with Coke when they weren't drinking it straight. Coke was so synonymous with soda that we called all sodas Coke, a fact that Jennifer S., my significant other thirty years later, still dislikes.

We did not know then that Coke had always attached itself to America, and that looking at the history of Coke outlined a history of our country, such as how it branded itself the "temperance beverage" and sided with Prohibition. Beginning in the late 1870s, the Women's Christian Temperance Union began a campaign against alcohol that was widely successful. Soda companies stepped in to fill the gap created when people gave up alcohol, and in 1895 Coke declared itself on the side of temperance; by 1906 their slogan was "the Great National Temperance Beverage."

Coke's ads each year tried to capture the American mood.

In the '30s they claimed it was "wholesome" and "served in hospitals." During World War II Coke said that "no matter where you go" there's a big red sign near you, meant to remind you of home, which was, obviously, meant to remind soldiers stationed overseas of home, and all the good things associated with it. With the automobile boom following the war, Coke's slogan changed to "Along the Highway to Anywhere."

By 1969 Coke was proclaiming itself "the Real Thing," which Coke's then brand manager, Ira Herbert, said heralded a new direction that "respond[ed] to research which shows that young people seek the real, the original and the natural as an escape from phoniness." As part of the Real Thing campaign came the 1971 song "I'd Like to Buy the World a Coke." In '75 Coke was telling America to look up, and by 1986, when I began badgering Kevin Sloak over his taste in beverages, Coke Classic was advertising "Red, White & You" as a claim to our patriotism.

All of these advertisements conform to traditional values in some way, appealing to nostalgia and family. Hippies were seen by a majority of Americans as phony, anti-American, the culture that ran counter to what old white men believed. Coke was branding itself as wholesome, a drink that promoted temperance, that adhered to the family values of purity and hospitality, that celebrated "Red, White & You."

In contrast, Pepsi tried to advertise itself as a youthful brand, keeping up with cultural and social changes instead of adhering to nostalgia and nuclear values. Pepsi said that every new generation brought its own emergence, so they tried to appeal to youth in the '60s with "Now It's Pepsi for Those Who Think Young," and "Come Alive, You're in the Pepsi Generation." In 1984 Pepsi abandoned all pretense and claimed it was the drink of a New Generation, and all these advertisements appealed to a more liberal lifestyle, of newness, of thinking—and being—young.

We should have liked Pepsi. But we were hung up on our parents' politics. Coke was wholesome and nostalgic and American, which meant conservative in those times, as if we were still looking back at the '50s before all that counterculture shit came along. Conservative meant opposing the changing values of the times, conserving the beliefs that had served us all so far and would continue doing so.

It also meant opposing the Soviet Union, an idea which had been hammered and sickled into us at an early age, into our parents growing up in the '50s, when the two biggest kids on the block began to fill their arsenals with missiles that could change the very air we breathed. During elementary school they crawled under their desks to practice dying. Pepsi had sided with the Soviet Union, and so they were traitors, which meant we stuck to Coke and conservatism. Coke's ad from '75 had worked—we were looking up all right—only we were looking for missiles, and the end.

The Cola Wars weren't the only wars that pitted the US against the USSR. Cinema also showed the struggle between the two states. I've already mentioned *Wargames* and *The Manhattan Project,* but those came after years and years of Cold War movies, including *Dr. Strangelove, Ladybug Ladybug,* and *Duck and Cover,* a 1951 educational film that taught school children what to do in case of a nuclear attack, as if covering up would save them from an atomic bomb. Before that, both countries put out propaganda films, and though I haven't seen the Soviet ones, I know ours were meant to either scare us or convince the rest of the world we were a beacon of democracy and hope.

We also wanted the Soviet Union to be seen in the worst light. Our movies said so, from *Rocky IV* to *Red Dawn*, and TV did too. *MacGyver,* which I watched on Monday nights with my stepfather while he mixed his Evan Williams with Coke, often pitted MacGyver against the Soviets or East Germans, the enemies always depicted as angry men in blocky overcoats whom MacGyver easily outsmarted. In reruns, Rocky and Bullwinkle fought Natasha and Boris.

Besides the fake wars we saw on the screen, Reagan almost started a real war when he said that the Soviet Union had been outlawed forever and we would begin bombing them in five minutes. Nixon traded barbs with Khrushchev all through the Kitchen Debate, attempting to convince the world the United States was superior. LBJ used the "Daisy" ad to defeat Barry Goldwater, but it was designed to remind us all of the Soviet threat. In it, a little girl in a field counts the petals of a daisy; when she reaches nine, a man's voice begins the countdown to nuclear war, and when the voice reaches zero, a mushroom cloud fills the screen.

The Cold War sat in our classrooms as well, where the Soviet Union dominated our maps. Because it was all one color, we thought of the Soviet Union as one uniform country: cold and lifeless, full of hatred and jealousy for our American way of life. In our defense, we had been taught this. The Pledge of Allegiance before school and National Anthem at every sporting event instilled the kind of patriotism in us that excluded others. Our nation was under God, meaning blessed, as so many politicians would come to say. Starting as early as third or fourth grade, we learned about the evils of communism and the military might of the Soviet Union after World War II, how the Cold War bloomed from the ashes of Eastern Europe. By middle school everyone except Kevin Sloak said that if we lived in the

Soviet Union we'd pretend to be a communist as we climbed higher and higher in government, until the day we were Premier or Czar or whatever the hell they called it, then change everything. We'd change the country from communism to capitalism and we'd dismantle their missiles and flood the market with American music and Coca-Colas and win the culture war without ever firing a missile.

It never occurred to us that Gorbachev was trying something similar. The change from communism to capitalism came slowly and painfully, and none of us cared to know any of the details, though we saw the long lines at the grocery stores on the news and heard the reports of widespread anger. But it didn't occur to us this was happening to real people because we had already, in our minds, so far removed the Soviets from humanity they might as well be another species.

It also never occurred to us that we could do the same for our country. We could climb high in the ranks and dismantle our missiles and end the threat of nuclear annihilation, but we never saw ourselves as the problem. It was the Soviets, with their Siberia and fur suits, their hard bread and Pepsi-Cola, who wanted to wage war against us.

Nor did we know about perspective, and how differently we might see the world if we lived elsewhere in it, if we grew up saluting the Hammer and Sickle instead of the Stars and Stripes. We didn't understand how worldview is created from where we stand in the world, how if we stood somewhere else we'd have a different view, which is to say we didn't know what we had been taught wasn't true. We saw the Soviet Union as a drab, summerless state, all their energy turned toward destroying everything we held dear.

So to fight back, we hated Pepsi, since hatred was the only thing we owned, other than undying devotion to Jennifer S. We drank Cokes by the fistful, and we made fun of Kevin Sloak and his stupid Pepsi-Cola, which meant "stomach nuts."

It did not seem odd to us in the '80s that two companies would feud over cola. Nor that a cola could represent a country we hated simply by associating with it. Perhaps it was because we were still kids or perhaps it was because of our culture and the Cold War, but it was easy to dislike anything different from what we knew. Easy to claim as communist anything we didn't understand, easy to call communism evil, easy to define a country with some derogatory term that fit our worldview, not knowing where we stood influenced us. It was so easy to hate Kevin Sloak, with his trench coat and fingerless gloves, sitting by himself on the front steps of the school, drinking his Pepsi-Cola and eating his peanut butter sandwich with the crusts cut off. So easy to believe our social studies teachers, who had grown up fearing what might fall on them out of the sky. So easy to cling to conservatism and our choice of colas, so easy to see only the hills that ringed our small town. So easy to see only two choices and not the many we already owned.

Coke eventually won the Cola Wars. The Soviet Union broke up in 1991, and Pepsi lost their exclusive deal. They kept parts of it together but were dealing with multiple countries now instead of one. Their bottling plant was in Belarus. Their ships were stranded in the Ukraine, which wanted a share of the cut. Pepsi put up giant billboards in Pushkin Square, but Coke still got in, and after only a few years they beat out Pepsi as Russia's most popular soda.

We should have rejoiced. But by then our hatred toward others had turned to the Middle East. I gave up sodas altogether and went straight to vodka, which I drank while watching the

Gulf War, worrying, once again, whether the end was coming. Soon I'd see enough of war to be sick of it. I woke too many mornings hungover, wishing for Sprite and chicken soup, for my mother telling me everything would be all right. Then the war ended, and we went back to work or school or lying alone in the darkness hoping the headache went away, knowing that it never would, that we would always fear the end of the world, that we would always be sick, would always need something like Sprite and chicken soup to heal our troubled souls.

Coke wanted to be seen as wholesome and family oriented, while Pepsi tried to appeal to the younger generation. They wanted to be the cool kids, to hang out with the Swatch watches and the acid-washed jeans and the feathered hair. Pepsi wanted us to see the world, but Coke said all we needed was right here. And since the world made us feel small and scared, we consumed our Cokes in the same way we swallowed conservative values—holding hard to the idea that the only way to win a fight was to build up our forces for the final battle. We held our hatred like rifles. We stoked our fear like fire and waited for the end, knowing God was on our side.

Thirty years later I found out Jennifer S. drank Pepsi. Her whole family did. Her father mixed his Canadian Mist with Pepsi. Sometimes Jennifer stole a sip from it on the Saturday nights when his friends came over to play cards. I have to admit that when she told me this, I felt a small twinge of betrayal. I called her a communist, but she understood the fear I felt, and so forgave me. The next day we went to a soda shop where she drank a Cheerwine and I drank a Big Red, neither of which are bottled by Coke or Pepsi. As if we had more than two choices. As if we could drink our sodas without fighting or fearing the end of the world. As if we could buy each other a coke, and drink it in perfect harmony.

# Optimism

This morning I wanted to buy a book about space travel, but the cold outside depressed me. Even the library seemed too far away for any expedition, so I stayed in bed remembering summer nights looking up at the stars. All the world seemed wild in those days, when I understood so little of everything. In our sixth-grade science book, men with abbreviations and credentials after their names suggested that when the sun grows too close for our comfort, we might colonize Saturn's moons. Mars might hold some semblance of life, and even Jupiter, more than one '70s scientist theorized, could harbor a safe haven under its gaseous clouds.

Other things those scientists said were that the seas with all their size could house a hundred billion homes. That in some future architecture we could build skyscrapers to scrape not only the blue sky but the stars we once craned our necks to see, imagining what it might be like living somewhere else, far beyond our own eyesight. We might build ships that could sail to distant solar systems—and what child has not imagined meeting an alien evolved from something other than apes, something so strange as to be wondrous?

In science class I learned that the earth's core was as hot as the sun's surface and that some planets were so cold that even the air was ice, but in that hopeful time those scientists assured me we would overcome whatever problems the future presented, and when the maintenance men painted the rusting gym equipment bright red, I believed them.

All science was hopeful, it seemed. Roy G. Biv taught me to memorize all the light we can see, and the planets were no more complex than My Very Entertaining Mother Just Served Us Nine Pizzas, those mnemonic devices designed to help us understand the world outside our windows.

Even the impending nuclear war was no problem, approached scientifically. If we had not yet advanced enough to make it to Saturn, we could live deep underground, at least until we found a way to clean up the radioactive mess, which made me wonder, looking out the winter windows, how cold the world could get when struck with that much fire. We would harness the power of the Earth's insides to create our haven, and here I imagined a hobbit-hole, safe from nuclear harm, though I did wonder, hiding under my covers, why we didn't just use the fire of nuclear fuel to warm us, or why we didn't stop the missiles before they burned the world.

But now, driving to the library forty years later through the honk and exhaust of the cold morning traffic, I'm reminded we're running out of room. The Kansas sky is big above me, but in the ground below me missile silos aim their spears at the stars, and satellites circle all through space. The oceans are too plastic-filled to house fish, much less humans, and my middle-aged skin feels too tight, like a promise I've been waiting on since 1979. Last night at the symphony, I listened to a 160 people singing Handel's *Messiah,* the "Hallelujah" chorus banging off the curved walls and coming back down to us. In the words reigns a hope for the future, which made me wonder when I became so pessimistic. Maybe I'm still waiting on those promises, because instead of the mysterious cosmos I once fantasized about, I can only envision a declining earth. On social media every day, I read about what a ruin the world is turning into. Some man in Florida sells crystal meth in an energy drink, and I know about it in Kansas the next day. A colony of bees collapses in Australia, and suddenly we're worried about all life on earth. The seas are warming, and scientists wonder now whether we'll even be able to stay here, much less reach out to the stars.

I'm not saying there's nothing to be worried about, but surely something of that once-envisioned future is still possible. I lived through all the fear and failure of the '80s too, the movies in which missiles launched from the Kansas prairie or secret codes led to nuclear countdowns, but recently scientists have found a way to produce a mineral that eats carbon dioxide, which could be a way to curb global warming. A drawing on a 73,000-year-old rock may be the earliest human art, showing how even in our infancy we wanted something to outlast our own lives. Water has been found on Mars, reigniting dreams of colonization, and the oldest stars at the heart of the universe, scientists believe, might mark our beginning.

What I'd like to believe is that those scientists in the '70s were right. In looking to the future, I'd like to believe some of those words I heard last night have escaped, and when they reach the vast blackness of space, someone will hear them, someone just learning that Saturn has over sixty moons, each as beautiful and varied as a note of music. Some alien child is drawing, right now, pictures of a planet he's never seen. His own planet has somehow survived the wars and rumors of wars, the corporations and capitalism, and the houses he draws—small white squares with a triangle roof, round yellow sun tucked in the corner above the black birds winging their way overhead—will seem strange and wondrous when he shows it to his parents, who will hang it on whatever passes for a refrigerator in that world. And then they'll walk out into an atmosphere we might never understand and look at the night sky, humming in all its vastness. The father will point out a distant speck of light.

"Someday we'll go there," he'll say, and for the rest of the boy's life, he'll believe it.

# Right Here, Right Now

In 1989 I had no idea who Santayana was, nor why Billy Joel was saying goodbye to him in "We Didn't Start the Fire." I didn't know Santayana once said, "Those who cannot remember the past are doomed to repeat it," but I had seen *Full Metal Jacket* and heard that the dead know only that it is better to be alive, which is a reasonable facsimile of Santayana's other famous quote that only the dead have seen the end of war. In the movie, Matthew Modine says his version while his character looks at a pile of corpses, which means it should have weighed on us long after the scene ended, but in my small Arkansas town we were all too busy quoting the Vietnamese sex worker who says "Me love you long time" to focus on any philosophical messages the movie portrayed.

This might be a metaphor for my teenage years—misinterpreting the messages in everything around me, including the lyrics of the music I listened to or the changing political climate. That November of '89, the Berlin Wall would come down, and an air of democracy, like the Scorpions' 1991 song, "Wind of Change," would sweep across Eastern Europe, but I didn't know for years what the Scorpions' song was about, only that I wished it would have been around in 1989 because it was slow enough I could have danced close to Jennifer S. at our high school dances but fast enough we wouldn't have had to calcu-

174

late, through some trigonometry only a teenager could explain, exactly how close we should be to each other's body.

"We Didn't Start the Fire" was recorded in July and released in September, two months before the Berlin Wall cracked, so Joel didn't know, when he was cataloguing the historical events of his life, how the future would go. This may be why he ends the song by saying the Cola wars have gotten to him, which is either a reference to Coke and Pepsi battling for supremacy in the soda market or a mispronunciation of *Cold War*. Either way.

Two years later, when "Wind of Change" came out, I wouldn't know about the failed coup attempt in the Soviet Union that spurred the song's creation, or that Mikhail Gorbachev, because he opened his country to the West, was widely hated by the old Soviet guard. The children of tomorrow share their dreams in the song, but my dreams at that age were more concerned with fleshly delights than any political movements, and they were too full of desire to share with anyone other than another consenting adult.

Because of this character flaw, call it something empty inside me or a need for companionship, there were many songs I missed the meaning of. Despite listening to "We Didn't Start the Fire" a hundred times on high school basketball trips, the history lesson eluded me. I didn't know Joel was born in 1949 and was forty in 1989, when the song was released. It's obvious the song is a list of all the history that shaped those of us in America into what we were in the late '80s, but who knew, in my small Arkansas town, of the significance of Dien Bien Phu, a name I'd never heard of even in history class because we were too busy learning about American exceptionalism.

Nor had I heard of Zhou En-Lai or children of thalidomide. I might have watched *The Bridge on the River Kwai* with my World War II veteran grandfather, but that might also have been *Shane* we watched, since he liked westerns and shied away from war movies for reasons he wouldn't go into, likely having to do with having seen war firsthand. I knew about Little Rock only because my stepfather's National Guard unit had been activated during the Little Rock Central High School integration of 1957. He was sixteen at the time, having lied about his age to enlist. In 1989 I was barely older than the high school students he was sent to protect, and hearing the story about how he was activated, how the United States came to blows over segregation, states' rights, and our own inherent bigotry and hatred, made me wonder what I was going to do with my life, but luckily the song ended. Prince came on, partying like it was 1999, and everyone sang along in the high school cafeteria, none of us realizing the song was about the end of the world, that everyone has a bomb, that parties weren't meant to last. Instead, the way we all do, all the time, ignoring the warnings right in front of our faces, we focused on the fun and not the finality. The balloons and not the bombs, because there's Jennifer S., standing alone, and surely she'll dance to a song that's all about living life to the fullest in the last few minutes before the world ends.

Despite my blindness to popular song lyrics, I was somewhat aware of the state of the world. I knew, even before Billy Joel began to write about fires and who started them, that the United States and the Soviet Union were fanning fires that might burn us all. The early '70s had seen a slightly better relationship between the two countries, but in the late '70s the Soviet Union began aiming SS-20 missiles at NATO targets in Eastern Europe. To counter the deployment of the Soviet SS-20, NATO forces set up Pershing missiles in Germany, which meant all of Eastern Europe was bristling with missiles.

The rest of the world was bristling as well. When Reagan became president in 1981, he began to build up US armed forces. He gave orders for new bombers, cruise missiles, and a six-hundred-ship navy. In 1983 Reagan tried to provoke the Soviets by sending his massive naval fleet to the North Pacific. Like two kids crossing imaginary lines, the US and Soviet Union antagonized each other: naval aircraft flew into Soviet airspace, prompting Soviet aircraft to violate American space. Of course, none of it was imaginary when the Soviets shot down a Korean airliner, thinking it was an American spy plane.

It was a dark time. That same year, in September, a Soviet computer glitch came close to sending the missiles into the sky. In November the US would alarm the Soviet Union with a realistic simulation of a NATO nuclear attack.

The music reflected the time, even if I didn't realize it. "Everybody Wants to Rule the World" by Tears for Fears told us how bad things were, that we had turned our backs on mother nature, that the surveillance society would always find us, that nothing ever lasts forever. But instead of listening to the warning about the dangers inherent in power, and the greed that often accompanies it, we chose to focus on the part about nothing lasting forever, making the most of freedom and of pleasure. After all, Prince had already informed us of that factoid.

Nena's "99 Red Balloons" tells the story of toy balloons, released by two friends at the break of dawn, that inadvertently bring about the end of the world. The balloons are erroneously reported as UFOs, which causes a mad scramble of fighter jets by generals on both sides. The resulting show of force brings about war, and the war ends the world, but thinking how easily the world might end—as it almost had in 1983—was too much, so we focused on the red balloons floating in the summer sky and not how something as simple as a floating toy might open the gates of hell.

"Burning Heart," by Survivor, released on the soundtrack to *Rocky IV*, sets up two worlds colliding, rival nations. The rest of the song is a vague, uninteresting collection of generic metaphors, with the exception of the line asking if it's East versus West or man against man. In the movie, Rocky, representing America, overcomes the superior firepower of Soviet Ivan Drago, played by Dolph Lundgren. The Soviets also begin chanting Rocky's name, as if he's won them over and they've realized the errors of not being American, so we left the theater throwing punches in the air and believing, in the event of nuclear war, that we would overcome the supposedly superior firepower the Soviets had aimed at us. *Rocky* was always about the underdog, and since the song was sung by a band named Survivor, we chose to believe that we would not only survive a nuclear war but win.

"We Didn't Start the Fire" is full of references to the Cold War and the threat of annihilation. Sputnik being launched by the Soviets led to the Space Race, but we didn't know as teenagers how much a satellite scared everyone in 1958. The fact that the Soviets could launch a satellite into space meant they could launch missiles to America, which made everyone look up at the sky. There are also lines in the song referencing the H bomb, the Bay of Pigs Invasion, and of course the all-consuming fire that it seems no one started, but none among us could focus on the fear those lines were supposed to elicit when there were references to space monkey and hula hoops, which meant, in our minds, the song was supposed to be fun.

I'll say now we'd had enough of fear. We were tired of being scared, of being told the world will end by men in suits who've poured over every inch of the Bible but somehow still obsess over the end instead of all the good things we're supposed to be doing before our end.

In other words, we didn't want to hear it in our music as well.

I keep using the word *we* because it seemed we all felt that way. By *we*, I mean middle-class white males, the kind who, because they were so scared as boys, grow up to be men always in favor of attacking any enemy. Riding home from basketball games on the school bus, having lost again to a team much taller than we were, music was our only reprieve from feelings of inadequacy. Jennifer S., despite my undying devotion, never wanted to sit with me in the back of the bus where my inappropriate fantasies might be fulfilled, so I was forced to listen to Survivor or Tears for Fears.

I'm also listening to Ozzy going off the rails on his crazy train, a song that says we are heirs to a cold war that isn't fair. It implies the wheels are coming off, that everything is inevitable, but there's still that cool Randy Rhoads guitar riff, and Ozzy's crazy-ass voice to help us ignore the inevitability of it all. I'm listening to Kate Bush sing "Breathing," about an unborn baby afraid of nuclear fallout. But Bush's voice is so beautiful it's hard to believe the bombs could fall, so instead I think of Jennifer S. at the front of the bus in her cheerleader uniform breathing the same air I am, with only minor traces of radioactivity in it. I'm listening to Queen's "Hammer to Fall," about growing up tall and proud in the shadow of a mushroom cloud, but since I am neither tall nor proud, I pretend the shadow of the mushroom cloud doesn't apply to me either. I'm fast-forwarding through Men At Work's "It's a Mistake," not yet fully understanding how close a mistake came to ending us all in 1983, and when I get to U2's "New Year's Day," I'm imagining it's actually about a party. When I hear Weird Al's "Christmas at Ground Zero," I am reminded we can make fun of both Christmas songs and the fear of the end. Or maybe he is making fun of our own short-sightedness, but I like the song because it says we can laugh at what scares us, and that, along with ignoring what we can't laugh at, gets me through the '80s in the same way music gets me through the interminable bus rides.

It seems we had a lot of time to listen. We took buses everywhere. In the mornings my brother and I waited in the cold and rode to school looking out the windows at the frosted world, listening to the *Thriller* album or *Pyromania* or *Metal Health*. We rode buses to basketball games and football games and track meets, all of us packed tight as on a train, a crazy one, where Michael Wilkins always had the newest cassettes and the girls made mixtapes for the boys they liked. On the way to the games we listened to Michael Jackson singing "Billie Jean" and thought about the word *lover,* or Prince and the girl wearing the raspberry beret; on the way home, after losing again, as the headlights of passing cars highlighted us there in our aloneness, we put in U2 singing "With or Without You" and worked our way into such despair we wanted the end of the world.

Friday nights we stayed up late to watch NBC's *Friday Night Videos,* a show for those of us with only three TV channels who didn't yet get MTV but still wanted to be part of the music world. We weren't yet old enough to drive, and all the anxieties of being a teenager afflicted us, so music became our emotion. Def Leppard's "Hysteria" could have been about feeling or fire, since it made us feel both, and I'll say now that's what we wanted: for our feelings to burn the world as hard as they were burning us. Watching videos late at night, my parents asleep in the other room, sound turned down so as not to wake them, I wanted the world of "Sweet Dreams" by the Eurythmics, that synth-pop, color-coded world where everyone is always looking for something. We all wanted to travel the world and the seven seas, if only to get out of here. We all wanted to be abused, and it occurred to me we also wanted to be abusers because the world was both.

"Love Is a Battlefield" confirmed this suspicion with its simple declaration that we would move from heartache to heartache. "Do You Really Want to Hurt Me" asked a simple question about desire, "Every Breath You Take" taught us it was okay to obsess over someone who had left us, and "Total Eclipse of the Heart," with its powder kegs and sparks and love in the dark, showed how easy it was for all our emotions to blow up.

War, we came to understand, was only another emotion. Like love, it made us who we were. We didn't know then that all our emotions are conflicted and easily confused and constantly under fire; we only knew we wanted to feel normal, even if we didn't know what that meant. We didn't realize it was normal, in the world we lived in, for the threat of war to always be there, or to believe, in such a world, that love was synonymous with hurt. We didn't want to be afraid, constantly looking at the skies, feeling like we would die at any moment, but the music of the time convinced us that love was a battlefield. That those who love you want to hurt you. And in a world where it was so easy to confuse love with war, how easy then would it be to embrace them both?

I also remember "Tainted Love" by Soft Cell and "West End Girls" by Pet Shop Boys. "Hate Myself for Loving You" by Joan

Jett and "I Melt with You" by Modern English. "Private Eyes" and "Under Pressure." "Owner of a Lonely Heart" and "It's the End of the World as We Know It," all of which had at their heart one extreme or the other and sometimes both. "West End Girls" divides the world into East and West at the same time it divides boys from girls. "Under Pressure" claims there's terror in knowing what the world is about, while "Private Eyes" are watching your every move. Modern English says we'll melt together when the end comes while Yes claims owning a lonely heart is better than owning a broken one, but, like love and war and waiting for the end, it's easy to confuse the two, even in the lyrics of the songs.

It might also be time to mention how around this time "God Bless America" began pouring out of the mouths of politicians as if He loved us more than any other country, which meant, in the minds of many, that we could do whatever we wanted, since we had His divine blessing. Or I could count the number of movies in which the action stars of the period—Chuck Norris and Arnold Schwarzenegger and Sylvester Stallone and Clint Eastwood—beat back forces that wanted to destroy us, usually single-handedly, and how we loved them for it. I could mention the Lee Greenwood country hit "God Bless the USA," which was released in 1984 and played at the Republican National Convention that year but which keeps coming back every time America falls under attack. In that song, Greenwood proclaims he would stand up next to you and defend her still today, because there ain't no doubt he loves this land, and when you love something, in this land, you immediately think of having to fight for it.

I don't think I need to mention hormones, how everything at that age—and here I mean both being a teenager and the time period of the mid-'80s—drove us to despair. Even "1999," that song about the ultimate party, was predicated on the idea that we could only party that hard if the end were near. "Little Red Corvette" says it was Saturday night so that makes it all right, but you need a love that's going to last, which, I'll say now, was all we were looking for—something that might last, whether love or the world we lived in.

It wasn't easy to ignore the rumblings of the world. Rap music had barely reached us in the form of Run-D.M.C., but we knew there was crack in the cities because we heard about it constantly in rural white Arkansas, the news sent to us, it seems now, as proof that there was nothing wholesome to be had in urban America. Our parents were divorcing at alarming rates. The savings and loan scandal had milked millions from their life savings, and though the news media still reported the spread of a deadly new disease called AIDS, the Reagan administration remained silent, perhaps because it was too embroiled in the Iran-Contra affair to take notice, or perhaps because, backed by the Moral Majority, who saw homosexuality as a sin, it didn't care.

AIDS became known as the "gay plague," but we were all plagued by indifference born of fear: of the wars that seemed to be everywhere, of this unknown new disease, of the poverty creeping up slowly on the middle class. Our parents, those that somehow still remained together, shook their heads sadly as they watched the nightly news, as if, it occurs to me now, they were engaged in the adult version of giving up, which is to grieve for a few moments before ignoring the offending article and going on with their lives.

As teens, we would not give up so easily, at least not when it came to grieving. Late at night I lay in my bed with my headphones on and felt sorry for myself. I did this often, listening to "With or Without You" or "I Want to Know What Love Is" and conjuring up a different version of myself, and the world. In this world, war was not the most prominent landscape, our church leaders were not obsessed with fire, and I was the kind of person who did not wish himself taller, or better looking or, at the very least, as confident as a character in a Prince song. This was a self-preservation technique, one I'll say we all engage in, believing that someday we will be able to sustain ourselves, that the world will ultimately not scar us forever.

It's also a lie. Those teen feelings of angst may be the truest of intuitions, the utter certainty that whatever we live through scars us always. And since we lived in utter despair, our own insides telling us we weren't enough and never would be, one more despair, even one dealing in the end of the world, was bearable, perhaps even preferable. The more angst we could carry, the better, like the scarves Danny Wilkins wore around his wrists (whispered rumor said because he had tried to slash them, which seemed, at that age, the ultimate in angst, propelling Danny to cult status). We were already bearing our changing bodies, our mood swings and melancholy, our inability to voice our desires toward the girls in our class except in crass ways, either by snapping their bras or that weird '80s phenomenon of "gleeking," which, if you've never heard of it, was, and there's no other way to say it, spitting on them. The end of everything was only one more burden to bear, and the only way to bear all of these burdens was to pretend they never existed. To wrap a load of scarves around your wrists or roll up the sleeves on your '80s trench coat and ignore it all, claim to be too cool to notice how awful everything was.

Imagine our confusion then when things began to get slightly better. The zeitgeist winds were a-changing, despite the awfulness of the last few years: the Challenger explosion, the

"We Are the World" song, the fact that no one seemed to realize Springsteen's "Born in the USA" was not a patriotic song and was instead critical of American culture.

In the Soviet Union, Mikhail Gorbachev was implementing programs to open up his communist country to the West, and it seemed the Cold War might finally warm. The Food and Drug Administration approved a blood test to detect HIV, meaning someone had finally recognized the suffering AIDS caused. The Iran-Iraq War ended, and Soviet troops began pulling out of Afghanistan.

In 1987 my older brother got a car, sparing me the interminable bus trips to school in the mornings and afternoons, my forehead pressed against the window while staring out at the brown pastures and listening to Queen's "Is This the World We Created?" or Crowded House singing "Don't Dream It's Over." Instead we listened to Escape Club's "Wild, Wild West" or the Nails' "88 Lines About 44 Women."

That same year East German police were beating people at the Berlin Wall because they snuck close enough to listen to Genesis and David Bowie and the Eurythmics, whose sweet dreams wanted to travel the world and not be stuck behind a wall. A year later Springsteen would play in East Berlin and tell the crowd of a hundred thousand that he hoped all barriers would be torn down.

During our basketball trips, the cold Arkansas night blacking the windows of the bus, we listened to "We Didn't Start the Fire" but only tried to memorize the words, not decipher what they might mean. We might have realized we already had too much history inside us, but I'll say now we knew there would be more words that came after the end, because there would be more history. It looked as if, after all, we might survive, that, like Rocky, we had beaten the evil Soviet Empire. Our parents had survived the recession of '87 and might even have enough money to send us to college, so by the time I was a senior I began to believe there would be more history to come. I believed the world would not end itself, music would get better, and I would someday leave the little town behind. All my insecurities would fall away, and I would become the person I had imagined in my room late at night, the one not forever scarred by the world we live in. I would find someone like Jennifer S., and we would, somehow, build a better world.

My first year of college, the most played song on college radio was "Right Here, Right Now" by Jesus Jones, a song that says we are waking up from history. It says right here right now, there is no place I'd rather be. The song was inspired by events in Europe in the late '80s, the Perestroika and Glasnost of the Soviet Union, the breaking down of the Berlin Wall. That spring of 1991, American forces won the Gulf War, which seemed to be about stopping the spread of a despot in the same way we had once stopped Hitler. "Wind of Change" claimed there was a new wind sweeping across the world, and with the victory in the Gulf and the collapse of the Soviet Union, we all felt it.

Then Grunge came along, and we all bought flannel shirts. I pined for a girl who ended our relationship prematurely by listening to Pearl Jam's "Black," and then Nirvana told us to nevermind. That with the lights out, it's less dangerous. Here we are now, they said, entertain us. The twenty-four-hour news coverage of the Gulf War entertained us, but when it ended, my roommate and I went back to watching cartoons. Late at night we turned up the music loud enough to block out everything else, which is, I'll say, what we've always done: turn up the volume loud enough we don't even hear what the song is about, as long as it entertains us. The nightly news lasted only thirty minutes when I was a child. Now we have stations that blast the news at us all day, and I'm not sure we have the stamina for that, as outrage only lasts so long before it turns to despair.

Or maybe "Right Here, Right Now" meant the world could end at any time. The "Wind of Change" could have been a Cold War wind blowing around the ashes of the past. None of those songs could have foreseen the future, despite Billy Joel trying to outline the past. No one knew that ten years later we would return to the Gulf, only this time the war would not be quick and decisive. We would enter Afghanistan like the Soviet Union once did, raising concerns about who we were, and whether we were, ultimately, as evil as those we once hated. No one knew how long the images of the Twin Towers falling would play in our heads, like a song we rewound again and again on our little Walkmans, which makes me think of Joel singing "After we are gone, it will still burn on and on (and on and on and on and on)."

I also keep returning to Tears for Fears singing "Welcome to your life. There's no turning back." And Crowded House telling us not to dream, it's over. And Men at Work saying we'll send a card and flowers after we've ended the world.

"99 Red Balloons" wants to find one souvenir, just to prove the world was here. Springsteen's out by the refinery, in the shadow of the penitentiary. Prince, despite the partying, asks Mommy why everyone has a bomb. U2 tells us this is the golden age, and gold is the reason for the wars we wage. Only Weird Al approaches the end of the world with a sense of humor, and a metaphor that's hard to miss, when he says, "We can dodge debris while we trim the tree, underneath the mushroom cloud," which means, of course, that nothing, not even the hope of Christ's birth, lasts forever in the face of humanity's desire to self-destruct.

Out of all the references in "We Didn't Start the Fire," close to half are about war in some way. Many are about the failure of leaders, or the hope they brought to the future. Another sizable portion mentions books, music, and pop culture of the time, which is fitting since the song itself has taken a place in our pop culture pantheon. But the almost equal divide between war and pop culture can only mean that in our country war has become part of our culture, and everything else is made up of the small moments we remember, in the few times we weren't afraid.

But we didn't notice it then. Or we chose to ignore it. Or we had other important things on our minds, like Jennifer S. who, thirty years later, I live with. The song ends with Joel unable to take it anymore, but the truth is we always find a way. No matter how bad the world gets, we preserve ourselves, either by ignoring what we can't bear or by choosing to believe we are different people, living in a different world. I'll say it's the only way we can sustain ourselves. That we are forever scarred and torn, and any wall we tear down is replaced by another, brick by brick. That the long arc of history might bend toward justice, but it's slow in coming, and hard to see, like the far curve of the earth, which would be easy to believe is flat, if the music we listened to didn't always come back to us.

# Cold

It had been snowing for hours when we left in the late afternoon, rifles slung over our shoulders and my dog dancing through the drifts. We went down through the front yard and across a frozen road and climbed the barbed-wire fence, our hands cold on the steel posts, wires humming with tension. The snow fell across the field like a screen coming down, and we stood with our breath like feathers in front of us. What leaves were still left on the trees turned in the slight wind and the same wind stirred the same snow at our feet and swirled it in the air and we stood listening to the sound of the cold coming down around us, which may be the sound of our own silences.

When the rabbit sprang up at our feet, Thomas raised his rifle. The report ricocheted to the far hills and back, though it sounded subdued by the snow. Already it seemed we were isolated. We could see a dark line of trees on the ridge above us and the dark ribbon of road that wound around our houses as it veered off toward town, but out here we were alone. We came to the woods to be alone, crossed fields and streams in search of solitude. This was the mid-'80s, and everyone was afraid. We were stuck still in the Cold War. It surrounded us like the air that afternoon. It got inside us, into every crack and crevice. It got under our clothes. Reagan was threatening to shut down the institute where my parents worked, and he was threatening, with his rhetoric, to bring us closer to war. My parents were angry and afraid, and often they allowed their emotions to overcome them. Thomas's parents did too. During the dark of movies, we'd hear the clipped sentences that meant the anger had aimed itself outward, the phrases that signaled a coming fight. Thomas would turn up the volume to drown out everything else, but out here we never heard such noises, nor were we forced to contemplate what they might mean.

The shot rabbit went squealing through the snow. We found it dying in a drift, tracked there by its bright blood. Shivering in the snow, it made a sound like a gate swinging open, or something shutting closed. Its eyes were half closed, conserving strength or meditating in its last moments, before Thomas took it by the back legs and bashed its head against a fence post. He tossed the limp body to the side of the road. We meant to find it on our return, but of course we never did. Way leads onto way, I've heard, and by the time we made it back we had our minds on other murders. We went across the field toward the dark line of trees, sliding through the snow as we went up and down small draws and across the little streams that crossed the field. Little birds blew backward in the wind. High above us hawks circled in the falling snow like small eclipses.

When we reached the line of trees, we turned to stare back across the fields. The wind was not as fierce where we stood at the forest's edge, looking back at the world disappearing behind us. It was easy at that age to think the world was disappearing. To think that everything was absolute, and whatever decisions were made for us would affect us forever, that we would grow old and still be haunted by the fear of what might fall on us from the sky. The snow came harder now, the wind whipping it around so that it seemed to circle. We might have been stuck inside a snow globe. We might have been shaken by larger hands, the way I am when I have too much to drink and look back on this scene to see two small boys standing on the edge of adolescence in a thin line of dark woods, wondering why they must always flee the sudden angers of adulthood. The borders of memory bend like the glass of a globe, but the whole world lies within, I sometimes think.

Sheltered from the wind and snow, we went around the dark trunks of the trees. We could no longer see Thomas's house behind us. The snow fell softly among the cedars. My dog slipped in and out of the trees with his nose stuck to the snow, bounding back every so often to shake his tail toward us. When we slid down the small ravines that ran through the woods, he would be bounding up the other side, just disappearing over the saddle, and we did not call him back for fear of breaking the silence.

At the old dump, we unslung our rifles. We had come here to shoot brown bottles and rusted cans and manual washing machines that had been abandoned years ago, before our houses were even built. We were aways coming upon old foundations deep in the woods, houses abandoned to time and tide, rutted roads like ghost tracks we could follow to find leaning chimneys and clapboard houses weathered by wind. We were always finding trash too, old refrigerators and washing machines and tin siding, detritus we could destroy. We imagined ourselves in a post-apocalypse as we lined up bottles half-emptied of whatever potion or poison they had once held and trained our rifles on them to watch them explode. We shot the hulls of the old washing machines and cast-iron stoves, the forgotten refrigerators and fine china, the mason jars and men's magazines, putting bullet holes through naked breasts after first flipping through to find all the forbidden parts.

I don't remember whether we came to destroy that day or were only looking for a few hours away from the exhalations of our houses, the long silences and the sudden angers and the overwhelming sadnesses of the time. Already we knew the world was coming to an end. The Soviet Union would destroy us any day, and even if they didn't, we knew our parents would soon be divorced. In that age every ending seemed the end, so we came here to seek solace in destruction.

We were struggling through one of the narrow ravines that cut through the countryside when my dog yelped. He had run ahead, and by the time we found him he had four gashes across his nose, already bright with blood. Before him a massive tomcat was hunkered down beneath a stunted cedar, hissing with its back up. It was the largest cat I have ever seen, one of those cats born wild, or else it had gotten away from whatever house it was raised in and gone feral. I thought at first it was a lynx or a bobcat. It had grown large in the woods, living on mice and rats and probably small rabbits—a cat that was no longer tame but had turned back to instincts that still lingered in its blood even after centuries of domestication tried to wipe them out. It was gray, one eye gone white. An old scar ran across its nose.

As we watched, my dog approached again, sniffing warily, as dogs will. In his short life he had only run across kindly cats that would curl up next to him and sleep, or bat at his tail when he wagged it. He got within a few feet and the cat charged, sinking its teeth into his nose. The dog went running backward, yelping, the cat latched onto his face, clawing at his eyes.

I don't remember who fired first, but I know now why. The dog was mostly Doberman and outweighed the cat by twenty pounds. But one of us fired, the report echoing through the snow to the far hills and back, and the cat flew sideways, where it lay for a moment, still hissing. It started to rise, and we fired again, both of us this time. We were carrying .22 caliber rifles, mine a Marlin semi-automatic and Thomas's an old bolt-action his grandfather had given him. From such a short distance we could not miss. We could see the bullets enter the cat's body, see the fur ruffled slightly, the holes blown through its skin. One shot tore out its white eye. Another almost severed a hind leg. It hissed again, though now it was weakened and bleeding, its eyes wild in the face of something it could not understand, as it slowly dragged itself through the snow, trailing its hind legs.

We followed, still firing. The dog came along, sniffing at the cat from a few feet away, cowering each time the rifles crashed. Eventually the cat stopped dragging itself and just lay hissing, but we kept putting rounds into it, laughing, for some reason that escapes me now, until one shot tore off the top of its head and it lay on its back with its mouth open. Another bullet went through its neck. The other eye blew out. The blood had stopped pumping, but its fur grew dark, and we kept firing into the coming darkness, our breath blown out before us.

When it was over, we stood in the ringing silence. The air tasted of gun smoke. The dog was still sniffing the cat's bloody body. His nose was gashed open, though already the edges were dried and crusted, and he wagged his tail while we inspected him. I kept thinking of the wild eyes of the cat as it sprung at the dog, which seems a simple enough explanation. We killed the cat because it bit the dog, because it looked as if it might puncture one of his eyes or rip off an ear. Its eyes were wild as winter and one of them was off-colored and we did not know what syndromes might swim through its blood so we shot it. This happened because this happened because this happened, simple equations one can track back to their beginnings. We killed the cat because it bit the dog. Because back behind us through the snow our parents were destroying one another. Because our leaders were on the brink of destroying everything. Because we were boys with guns who spent a lot of time in the woods and our families were falling apart and the world was falling apart and the dark and closeness of the forest seemed more comforting than the words that ricocheted off the walls of the places where we lived. Because we were at that age where every small mistake expands in the mind, where every failure seems massive, every ending final. Because we knew deep down there was something wrong with our lives that it would take years for us to recognize, and even more years to overcome. It was cold. We were at war. There were satellites above our heads and missiles below our feet, so we shot at everything.

We threw the cat beneath a cedar tree for burial. When we left the woods, it was snowing harder. Crossing the open fields, the wind blew the snow in our faces. My hands and feet were cold the way they can only get after a long time walking through snow, and though the cold had sunk all through me, I don't remember wanting to go home, just that the day would stretch into night while we kept walking. We had walked a long ways, and still had a long ways to go. We had not seen the sun all day, and now even the gray sky was turning dark as night closed in.

We were almost back at Thomas's house when we stumbled upon the idea that the cat might have been rabid. We stopped in the snow. The dog was shivering, instincts telling him he should not be out here, should be searching for shelter. The blood had dried black on his nose, and for a moment we looked at one another, wondering which way we would go.

With the porch lights in our sight, we turned around and began walking back. The snow had covered our tracks by the time we reached the woods again. It took us a long time to find the cat, searching the stunted cedars along the ravines. The body was already stiff with the cold. Thomas worked on one side, me on the other, sawing at its head with our pocketknives. Our small saws stuck in the cold bone. One eye was still intact, hanging from the empty socket.

When we finished, we turned and walked back toward our houses carrying the dead cat's head. It was too large to fit in our pockets and we had no gloves so we carried it in our cold hands until they were too numb to feel anything. When my hands started hurting, I passed the head to Thomas, and when he could no longer move his fingers he passed it back, one eye swinging on its sinews hanging from the empty socket.

At Thomas's house the porch light was still on. His mother's car was in the driveway. From inside we could hear voices, talking normally. When the roads cleared, we would call the vet and have the head examined, find out if my dog would have to be put down in a few days, if something even then was swimming in his blood from the bite. Thomas's mother stuck her head out the door and called for Thomas to come in, and I'm sure she offered me a ride or asked me to spend the night, but I walked home alone. It was dark now, the night thickening around me. From a long ways away I could see the porchlight on at my house. I stood at the top of the hill for what seemed a very long time, watching the light pool on the ground and the shadows of my family passing back and forth in the front room. I looked for stars, or the satellites I knew were swimming above my head. I knew soon someone would call them into action, but I couldn't see anything because it was still snowing, and very cold.

# The Sadness Scale, as Measured by Stars and Whales

It's easy enough to find, sadness, for there are so many stories of it disseminated on social media we might all stay quivering in our small rooms for as much time as we have left. In only the last week, besides the politics and polemics, the pipe bombs and opioid epidemic, I've thought about the fact that we live on a world where sunlight causes cancer, and a large number of Australian koalas have an STD. I've read that several times in our long and polluted history, we've managed to catch water on fire, and everyone you see today is someone who just hasn't died yet.

I know there are enough nuclear weapons in our arsenals to keep the earth burning for a thousand years, long after all the time capsules we've buried to speak to our future selves should have been opened, and there's a thought: how often we record ourselves, through pages or pictures, for posterity, afraid as we are of endings.

The nearest any other planet ever gets to Earth is around 160 million miles, and no one knows how big the universe really is or how it began or where it ends. No one knows if the sounds we spoke back when we were crawling out of caves are still rebounding into space, if someone might still hear them.

Most laugh tracks were recorded in the '50s, which means you're hearing dead people laugh when you watch a sitcom to ease the tension of your life or political leanings. That star you saw last night is likely dead too, and in all our sweeping of the universe, we've never found a sign we're not alone: not a signal or song from any planet, and despite the vastness of space, it's a little depressing to think how alone we are as we careen through the void.

One day your mother put you down and never picked you up again, and your children will never again be as young as they are right now. The smell of fresh cut grass is the grass trying to heal itself after you've cut it, and that smell after a rain is the way the world really smells, which makes me wonder why it can't always be like that, why we have to wait and wait for what we really want and afterward wish it were still that way.

There's a whale in the Pacific Ocean that sings at such a high frequency no other whales can hear it. Scientists have been monitoring it for over twenty years, and for all that time, it's been alone, still hoping someone is listening. Speaking of singing, every year on the anniversary of its arrival, the Mars Rover sings "Happy Birthday" to itself, millions of miles from anyone, and if that doesn't send some wind sweeping across the ocean of your insides, I don't know how to reach you.

Every day, it seems, there's a new loneliness loose in the world. Last week I read about a turtle whose shell had been fractured, so the zoo made a wheelchair out of Legos. Watching it crawl around, I cried like a child. Here was something so beautiful it hurt, like the memory of my grandmother, in the days before she died, saying she didn't like the color of the curtains in her hospital room.

There's also the unbearable sadness of school shootings, the systemic violence and oppression, the men who grease the wheels of government with their greed and the chance the Cold War is coming back, but even without the wars and the worry and all the horrors we hear about every day, we carry too much weight. Our thin skins can't even keep out the weather, much less the changes in our atmosphere. I try to remember the last time I picked up my grown daughters, and I might as well be searching the vastness of space.

Still, the search is worth it. Out there, past the bright unbroken stars of what we remember, is what we do not know. And somewhere in the asteroid belts of our lives lie the fragments we are forever trying to piece together to understand what it means to walk around on this good earth.

There's the warmth of your mother's hand on your forehead, the coolness of the other side of the pillow. The fresh spill of snow that means no school today, the brightness of the world when we get just a minute to look at it. The tickle of carbonation on your upper lip from the Sprite right after a swim the year you turned eleven and learned about girls. Or boys. Or football or music or whatever you learned that year, still skipping across the hot summer cement, before acne and awkwardness set in.

And even that wasn't so bad, remembering the way your date looked at prom your junior year. Or the way your whole small town stood and cheered when your basketball team ran onto the court to the tune of whatever song was popular then or the way on summer nights you circled town like the stars spinning in the night sky or the way everyone told you to stay cool when they signed your yearbook.

At the end, I bet you'll remember the sound of the garbage truck on the street in the morning with something like nostalgia. You'll remember your first wife putting on her makeup, mirror still steamed from the shower, before all the growing apart began. You'll see again your father, and I'll remember the last time I held my daughter, the time I put her down and never picked her up again, except to say, when she was over-whelmed by all the anger in the world, that I was still there, that whatever happened my voice would still be searching for her through space.

I'm trying to see stars the same way I did as a child, won-dering not what's out there for me, but just what's out there. I'm trying not to imagine dead solar systems but that light still leaks from them long after they are gone. I want to smell the air after the rain and be thankful for that moment, no matter how long I have to wait for it to come again. For every injustice in the world, there is a spider crawling up a waterspout. For every anger, an echo. For every wrong, a right now.

You'll never be as young as you are right now, which makes right now the best now. If our parents put us down and never picked us up again, it's because the weight of their worry grew too much, the same as we'll be unable to carry our children to completion, the same as we'll be unable to walk with them into the wherever.

But what beauty it will be to hear those who are long dead live again, not the canned laughter of some stupid show but what waits for us in the wherever. I hope if we do end up burn-ing the earth that aliens will see the smoke from the fire and perhaps make different mistakes than ours. Or none. Or all of them, and learn, before they begin the burning, so that when the light of our fire gets to them, they'll see only a night sky, our planet perhaps a little brighter against the darkness.

And sometimes I think of that whale and realize he's still singing, even if no one else is listening. It's beautiful, that song, the way it moves through the water of our bodies, where we are all alone. And the Mars Rover, singing to itself as well—some-one programmed that. Someone marked the milestones in its metric or electric or whatever it is the Rover runs on, like lines drawn in the Martian soil to measure its days so far from home, so far from where it came into being. I don't know what the song sounds like, but I know it is good. It is sad and slow and sweet, and it echoes all through the universe of my small heart.

# Acknowledgments

I wrote the essays in this book over a period of more than five years. Some of the earlier essays were written before I even began thinking about a book, and some of the later ones after I thought the book was finished. Some of the editors who originally published these essays have moved on. At least one of the journals is no longer in existence. The '80s are long gone, and breakdancing seems little more than a side note in history, but since the internet is forever, I'd like to thank the editors who gave these essays life: Kristin Tenor and Jacqueline Doyle, Melinda Lewis, Heide Weidner, Mary-Kim Arnold, Bruce Falconer, Giselle Firmino, Kristen Iverson and David Lazar, Wendy Wagner, Emma Komlos-Hrobsky, Leah Angstman, Aumaine Gruich and Ted Sanders, Donna Talarico and Rae Pagliarulo.

These essays previously appeared in the following journals or anthologies:

"Choose Your Own Adventure for '80s Kids," *Craft*
"Star Wars," *Smart Set*
"Left Turn at Albuquerque," *Under the Sun*
"The Full Moon," *The Rumpus*
"Candy Cigarettes," *American Scholar*
"Arc," *Qu*

"Morgue," *Don't Look Now* (edited by Kristen Iversen and David Lazar)

"Step on a Crack," *Nightmare Magazine*

"New Words for the New World," *Tin House*

"Breakdown," *Smart Set*

"Dead Baby," *The Coil*

"Cold Cola Wars," *Ninth Letter*

"Optimism," *Hippocampus*

"The Sadness Scale, as Measured by Stars and Whales," *Qu*

Besides the editors of lit journals, I'd like to thank my pre-editors—writer friends who saw some of these essays before their final form—who helped shape them into their final form. Sometimes this was direct intervention; in other cases I'm thanking people for their indirect support: phone calls late at night when we're doubting our abilities, emails to share good news.

Many thanks to Matt Fiander for his careful edits during "Storytime." I've lost the folder, Matt, but still remember where the big table is at Old Town. Many thanks to M. C. Armstrong and J. T. Hill, who fall into the second category, but only because of distance.

Many thanks to my editor at The Ohio State University Press, Kristen Elias Rowley. It was a pleasure to work with Kristen again, not only because of her kindness but also because she always helps me see my writing in a new way—my work is much stronger with her help.

I reserve the most thanks for Jennifer S., whom this book is dedicated to. But the dedication doesn't describe all the times she's read these essays, or listened to me read them, or listened to my tortured typing early in the morning, or any of a thousand things she's done simply because she cares. I owe you a Coke, Jenn.